На монте пут.

С обпе,

Диляна

MW01043366

The Politics of Muslim
Intellectual Discourse
in the West

To Constantin and Petar,
For Life!

The Politics of Muslim Intellectual Discourse in the West
The Emergence of a Western-Islamic Public Sphere

Dilyana Mincheva

sussex
ACADEMIC
PRESS
Brighton • Chicago • Toronto

Copyright © Dilyana Mincheva, 2016.

The right of Dilyana Mincheva to be identified as Author of this work has been asserted in accordance with the Copyright, Designs and Patents Act 1988.

2 4 6 8 10 9 7 5 3 1

First published 2016 in Great Britain by
SUSSEX ACADEMIC PRESS
PO Box 139
Eastbourne BN24 9BP

and in the United States of America by
SUSSEX ACADEMIC PRESS
Independent Publishers Group
814 N. Franklin Street, Chicago, IL 60610

and in Canada by
SUSSEX ACADEMIC PRESS (CANADA)

All rights reserved. Except for the quotation of short passages for the purposes of criticism and review, no part of this publication may be reproduced, stored in a retrieval system, or transmitted, in any form or by any means, electronic, mechanical, photocopying, recording or otherwise, without the prior permission of the publisher.

British Library Cataloguing in Publication Data
A CIP catalogue record for this book is available from the British Library.

Library of Congress Cataloging-in-Publication Data
Mincheva, Dilyana.
The politics of Muslim intellectual discourse in the West : the emergence of a Western-Islamic public sphere / Dilyana Mincheva.
pages cm
Includes bibliographical references and index.
ISBN 978-1-84519-765-0 (hbk : alk. paper)
    1. Islamic countries—Relations—Western countries. 2. Western countries—Relations—Islamic countries. 3. Islam—Relations. 4. East and West. I. Title.
DS35.74.W47M56 2016
303.48′2176701821—dc23

2015025066

Typeset and designed by Sussex Academic Press, Brighton & Eastbourne.
Printed by TJ International, Padstow, Cornwall.

Contents

CONTENTS

Acknowledgments

This text wouldn't have been possible without the four years spent as a doctoral student in the vivid, stimulating, and intellectually challenging environment of the Cultural Studies Department at Trent University (2009–2013). For creating this unique atmosphere I would like to thank the directors of the PhD Program in the mentioned period who took dedicated care of me as a doctoral student: Prof. Emeritus John Fekete and Dr. Alan O'Connor. Ever since then the Cultural Studies Department at Trent University has become a professional environment for me. I would like to thank my colleagues – Victoria de Zwaan, Emilia Angelova, Zsuzsa Baross, Ian MacLachlan, Jonathan Bordo, Ihor Junyk, Veronica Hollinger, Yves Thomas, Liam Mitchell, Liam Young, James Penny, Diana Manole, Hugh Hodges, Michael Morse, Rachel Cyr, Jeremy Bell, Gregory Kalynik, Gozde Killic, Jeremy Leipert, Troy Bordun, and Chad Andrews – for creating an exciting interdisciplinary environment that educates me every day in the courage of intellectual and ethical involvement with the public spaces and discourses of contemporary modernity.

Particularly, I would like to express my heartfelt thanks of gratitude to Dr. Davide Panagia whom I regard not only as a mentor but also as a role model, inspirational, supportive, and patient. I could not be prouder of my academic roots and hope that I can, in turn, pass on the research values and the dreams that he has given to me. I would like also to thank Prof. Emeritus Andrew Wernick, whose expertise, understanding, and vast knowledge in the field of sociology of religion added considerably not only to the writing of the following text but to my whole professional experience as a scholar of religion, culture and politics.

A very special thanks goes out to Prof. Emeritus John Fekete, without whose motivation and encouragement I would not have fought to finish this book project on time. He provided me with direction and support and became more of a mentor, and friend, than a colleague. It is through his persistence, understanding, and kindness that I am able today to see the final version of my book. I doubt that I will ever be able to convey my appreciation fully, but I owe him my eternal gratitude.

I would like also to express heartfelt gratitude to my colleague and friend, Jeremy Leipert, for the dedicated linguistic editing and comments on the entire manuscript. Thanks to him the book is written in a better English and its message is more communicative than I have ever hoped it would be.

I recognize that this research would not have been possible without the financial assistance of OGS, the Trent University Graduate Studies, the Department of Cultural Studies at Trent University (Teaching Assistantships), the financial assistance of the Doctoral Program in Cultural Studies at Trent University (Research and Travel grants), and the research funds of Canada Research Chair in Cultural Studies, and express my gratitude to those agencies.

Alexander Kiossev, Galina Goncharova and Boyan Znepolski are the three people from the Department of Cultural Studies in Sofia, Bulgaria, to whom I owe special gratitude for introducing me (many years ago) to the complex world of cultural theory and history. Their openness to intellectual experimentation and passion for research inspired me to become a scholar of cultural studies in the first place. Throughout the years their personal example has convinced me on numerous occasions that any cultural studies project worthy of its name involves commitment to complexity, contingency and imagination. Despite the fact that this book was written far away from Bulgaria and for topographical reasons far from Alexander, Galina and Boyan, their subtle intellectual presence is discernible on every page. I thank them here for inspiring me to embark on this journey and for being with me on it every step of the way. Simeon Evstatiev and Vladimir Gradev, the two Bulgarian scholars of Islam and religion, whose efforts to bridge what seems at moments unbridgeable and to comprehend what seems at moments incomprehensible, are the figures who have contributed generously to my formation and training as a scholar in the field of religion. I admire them and thank them for showing me what intellectual courage means in the face of political, spiritual and cultural ruin.

The design of the book cover I owe to my dear friend, the Bulgarian-Canadian artist Milena Doncheva. Her talent and sensitivity proves again and again that creative imagination is the most reliable bridge between realities marked with seemingly unsur-mountable difference. I am forever grateful that chance met me with Milena and that the design of the book cover turned into a precious and shared moment of creativity. I also thank the editors of Sussex Academic Press, and particularly Anthony Grahame, for the interest in my project and the careful and thoughtful comments that came along its realization. The final version of the book I owe entirely to him and his committed colleagues.

Finally, I would like to thank my parents for the support they provided through my entire life. Yet the presence of mind and soul for successfully finishing this adventure springs from the two people who *are* my life: my son Constantin, who came as a present at the very end of this writing project to teach me more than I could ever imagine, and Petar Enchev, my heart's companion, whose multiple talents converge in his passionate and graceful way of loving life and living love in every single moment of our existence. To them both I dedicate the book.

Introduction

The Damaged Notions of East and West

Maelzel's chess player

In "On the Concept of History", Walter Benjamin describes a weird automaton. A large-sized Turk with a hookah, who is actually a puppet, presents himself as an omnipotent chess player. This is possible because of a chess master, hunchback dwarf hidden underneath the chess table who navigates each move by pulling the strings of the puppet. The dwarf is invisible because of a complex system of mirrors, which makes the chessboard seem transparent and, in effect, hides the dwarf master. Johann Nepomuk Maelzel, who was, in 1769, the inventor of this chess machine described by Benjamin, was at the time a well-recognized German engineer focused primarily on inventing musical automatons (and despite the fact that he was also a bit of a showman, he managed to win the admiration of Beethoven in Vienna and later invented for him ear trumpets to aid the composer with his hearing loss). Certainly the presence of Oriental symbols, distorted bodies, technology, and puppet theatricality as well as the classical motif of the "ghost in the machine" evokes the Romantic aesthetics also responsible, as Edward Said claims, for the orientalism of the Europeans.

The puppet, Benjamin continues, represents "historical materialism" while the dwarf represents "theology," which is "small and ugly and must be kept out of sight." Benjamin further suggests that, in this game, historical materialism is "to win every time."[1] Whether this remark has been made with irony or as a criticism against historical materialism given Benjamin's well-known and widely commented theological preferences – Scholem, Schmitt, Rosenzweig – there is here, nonetheless, a peculiar insistence on history's triumphant certainty.[2] Probably because, as Maelzel's experiment suggests, theology is secretly guiding the triumph of history. Or, quite the opposite: probably because, as others have suggested, history has its own flow, structure, and directions.[3] Or mostly, because, as the work of Cornelius Castoriadis suggests,[4] history is made by the people as an utterly worldly affair; it is made by the people precisely *because they are capable of making, shaping, and altering the conditions of their lives, even if this does not always happen "as they please." Actually, Benjamin's writing reflects a historical moment – the insanity of Nazism – when history itself is, in one of its greatest performative defeats, reminding us – even though it could be against Benjamin's intentions – that history is a human affair and its making or un-making could be to the liberation, alteration, or destruction of all humanity.*

From a certain perspective, it is worrisome to equate history, a secular and worldly, human affair, with theology.[5] Not only because in this scheme history, as theology, may become a major vehicle of all kinds of hegemonic identity politics but also because such an equation prevents critical dismantling of anything deemed "secular," "historical," or "theological." Since they seem to be the same thing, all critique relevant to one of the terms is easily transferable to the other. Yet what distinguishes history from theology is precisely the secular element in the historical process, which is also intimately linked to human action, imagination, and creativity, and which, as understood here, happens in defiance of all domination. History's victorious triumph, to refer back to Benjamin, is neither due to its structure or flow, nor to its inherently theological nature, but rather to the fact that in its unexpectedness and unpredictability it is not tied to the rigorous court of Cartesian Reason, nor is it humbled by the submissive convenience of Piety.

The concept of history as a secular, human affair is important for the model of the Western-Islamic public sphere because history, understood as such, does not aim to deprive the world of its uncertainty and precariousness, nor does it participate in a truth-making process that lies outside human authorization through transcendalization. What is more, there is a performative and poetic moment in the historical that is also profoundly political, which means that the poesis and performativity of history stretch beyond the aesthetic confines of poetry and literature. *History* rather pertains to societies' capacity to imagine themselves and their enemies, to shape their present time and their future, and thus to change the direction of history, ultimately to their own benefit or destruction. The Western-Islamic public sphere, therefore, is a critical intellectual project that takes into account the reverberations and uncertainties of all controversial historical entanglements that define the domains of what is called *the West* and *Islam*. It is a project of intellectual critique inasmuch as critique's etymology is rooted in the Greek word *krisis* meaning to question, to interrogate (and it also means crisis), which defines a field of contention. Yet a practice of critique, in order to be also a poetical and historical practice, should be directed towards self-interrogation and self-critique, and this is truly the sense in which the Western-Islamic public sphere hinges on the intellectual work of critical Muslim intellectuals. Critical Islam, broadly defined throughout the whole book as the intellectual production of Muslims who were born and/or educated in the West, goes back to the fundamentals of the Islamic religion and questions them through historicization and de-transcendalization. As a controversial exercise yet one which is quite serious about its political commitments and social goals, critical Islam is a practice permanently in *crisis*, i.e. in the state of questioning, discussing, and periodically changing itself and its subject.

An important moment (to which I continually return throughout the book) for understanding critical Islam (and the whole project called the Western-Islamic public sphere) is that it does not aim to eliminate theology; being critical of religious dogma and grounding a critical project of reinterpretation in the worldly, secular domain of human action and thought does not mean the annihilation of religion. On the contrary, this attempt aims to *anthropologize* religion, namely to de-transcendentalize the omnipotent God of domination and submission, always beyond the reach of the human, and to see Him and His obedient servants as part of the complex historical flow. The Islamic subject, therefore, according to critical Islam, is a historical subject: someone who creates, alters, and destroys the conditions of his or her own life. In that framework one could object that Islam as a divinely revealed concept and perfect alterity is probably impossible. And yet, it is possible, critical Islam argues, and it happens in the only way anything could happen in the world – *in* history, *as* history.

Critical Islam is indeed a highly contested practice of religious interpretation. The distrust towards it springs from the feeling that the methodologies and commitments of critical Islam are too closely aligned with the compromised critical apparatus of Western social sciences and humanities.[6] And therefore they are tarnished by the Enlightenment legacy of thinking. From this perspective and very much against critical Islam, very often a somewhat cryptic return to dogmatic theology is proposed as an appropriate venue for locating new ways of critique. As Aamir R. Mufti claims, there is a widespread "mood" in current scholarship and theory that recognizes in religion as "belief, ritual, institution or identity" a means of healing "the shattered totality of life in modernity."[7] While I completely agree with the assumption that one should aim to go beyond the compromised legacy of the Enlightenment (mostly the one associated with practices of imperialism, hegemony, and racism), at the very least, however, the thing that an intellectual and critical mind should not do, in the process of disowning the past, is to subscribe to dogma. With regard to Islam, this Western academic tendency of distancing from the Enlightenment's critical apparatus often results in a *laissez-faire* attitude towards dogmatic practices.[8] At least two major consequences follow from here. The first is often uncritical advocacy or defense of the Islamic dogmatic praxis, which I believe ignores Islam's complexity, and the second is that the dogma becomes the measure for evaluating Islamic thinking, which, in turn and very much against the original intentions of the Western academics involved, reinforces the feeling that Islam is so radically different from "us" justifying its representation by conservative forces as the enemy of the West in a general sense. The Western-Islamic public sphere, I would argue, circumvents those two dangers without falling victim to forms of dogmatism associated with religion, nor eliminating (as hegemonic secularist narratives do) religion from the complex social lifeworlds. Critical Islam gives emphasis to various – and controversial – traditions of reformation in Islam, and precisely this aggregate that I call the Western-Islamic public sphere is a potential event of reformation. The reformation comes via the engagement of the homeless, liminal, in-between voices of the different Muslim intellectual projects that I discuss throughout the book.

This monograph, I hope, explains theoretically, and through analysis of artifacts, the importance of critical Islam for the emergence of an intellectual universe with high political stakes, namely the Western-Islamic public sphere. Given the above-mentioned heated debates around the public presence, recognition, and celebration of Islam in Western settings and the debates on secularism's hidden undemocratic agendas (and generally the exhaustion of the hegemonic Western archive), I realize that my project enters those discussions in a rather unconventional way. First, I maintain that the Western-Islamic public sphere is deeply rooted in secular praxis and thinking, inasmuch as critical intellectual work is always in essence historical – it is shaped by the movement of time and its dominant fashions and concepts. Yet, the Western-Islamic public sphere is not a secularist project inasmuch as secularism, as many have claimed,[9] is a regime of institutional metaphysics, which, similarly to dogmatic theology, obeys an external set of rules and regulations that strictly define what is to be called "religious" and what is to be called "secular." Equations between the secular, the secularist, and the theological, therefore, are misleading and my project operates beyond them. Second, the Western-Islamic public sphere equally deconstructs the orthodoxies of secularism and religion through the poetic praxis of intellectual critique, which is never a neutral task because it always intervenes in a field of heated disagreement. In effect, this is the reason why intellectual critique is always a political task. Finally, the Western-Islamic public sphere relies on intellectual imagination inasmuch as imagination is imbricated in the process of producing and/or altering the world but unlike other forms of authority – God, the King, the nation, the market, etc. – it is always internal to this process. In its always transformative and creative power, intellectual imagination rejects the logic of identity and it is therefore conceived here as the most powerful tool for escape from the pitfalls of all kinds of dangerous identity politics. Given my commitment to the role of public intellectuals in this arena, I have chosen to take on the poetics of the essayist.

Main Concepts

Secularization versus Secularism

The book is focused on a group of Diasporic Muslim intellectuals who are framing a critical intervention in dogmatic Islamic discourses – an intervention that I call the Western-Islamic public sphere but it could be seen also as an archive of homeless, dissident voices – that is neither orientalist/secularist nor Islamist/fundamentalist. An important claim that I make throughout the book is that the emergence of those new Islamic voices is part of a complex process of secularization of Islam which, in effect, is a new and somehow poorly understood phenomenon, or better yet, a phenomenon that codifies an emergent historical terrain. The secularization of Islam should not be mistaken with advocacy of secularism[10] because it is open and unfinishable – unlike secularism, which, as I wrote previously, pertains to the institutional structures and organization of society – by its very nature as a historical process. Secularization of Islam, as understood here, is linked to the desire of the Muslim voices under discussion to free themselves of dogmatically and religiously imposed constraints and to confront the consequences of encountering life in constant questioning of God: life without any safeguards. The cosmological abyss (put in poetic terms) that comes out of this lack of safeguards cannot be encountered once and for all; rather, this is a process that, in the personal and professional biographies of those Muslims, is intrinsically related to practices of critique that entail experimental and (self-)interrogative engagement with the social-historical. Even more, the critique generated by critical Islam, I argue, is a poetic encounter with the Islamic social imaginary of our times. Therefore, advocacy of secularism and secularization, in the context of critical Islam, should not be equated because secularism, as an institutional metaphysics, is one of the objects dismantled by the type of critique – which is *secular* – recommended by critical Islam.

Yet one of the main dangers of what I call secular critique may come with the closure of its horizon and its possible institutionalization and instrumentalization for the sake of undemocratic agendas. What I suggest here, as possible escape from this danger, is to think about the secularization process (in general and of Islam in particular) as incomplete and unfinishable. The point is not to explore in what ways the secularization of Islam could or should be completed (via intellectual or institutional processes) because the aspiration for completion itself, my argument suggests, is heteronomous. With critical Islam something more modest is at stake, a historical claim. In historical terms, secularization comes into being with the disruption of the religious apocalyptic world and, in effect, it signifies reorientation of the social imagination towards human finitude (towards mortality but also towards constant human [re]invention in a world deprived of existential guarantees) over a restricted condition of finality in the One Absolute and All-Signifying God. This is precisely the process reflected in the oeuvre of the new Muslim intellectuals in question. Their work – regardless of whether it is academic, literary, or related to public activism – deals with religion as a cognitive category, as an epistemological domain in itself. This allows critical Islam to identify and criticize (from the inside as far as all those intellectuals define themselves as belonging to the religious and cultural habitat of Islam) a certain number of religious practices and to explain their historical nature;

indeed, this historical perception of religion points to a shift in the framework of knowledge, which enables the understanding that religion in general, and Islam in particular, is one glorious and important human creation, among many.

Poesis and History

The recognition of religion as human creation is controversial and new to Islam. The type of secular critique that is inherent in the work of critical Islam is a result, I argue, of these new Muslims' continuous presence, education, and public roles in the West. A famous passage from Marx reveals the underlying secular politics of critical Islam (despite the fact that none of the intellectuals defines him- or herself as an overt Marxist):

> The basis of irreligious criticism is: *Human beings make* religion; religion does not make human beings. Religion is the self-consciousness and self-esteem of humanity which has either not yet found itself or has already lost itself again. But the *human* is not abstract being encamped outside the world. The *human is the world of humans*, state, society. This state, this society, produce religion, an *inverted world consciousness*, because they are an *inverted world*. Religion is the general theory of that world, its encyclopedic compendium, its logic in a popular form, its spiritualistic *point d'honneur*, its enthusiasm, its moral sanction, its solemn complement, its general ground of consolation and justification. It is the *fantastic realization* of human essence because human essence has no true reality.[11]

What Marx identifies as "irreligious criticism" refers precisely to humanity's ability to be in a constant state of poetic self-creation, or, put it in other words, to be confronting its own groundless nature, its abyssal essence. "Human essence has no true reality," Marx maintains, which means, basically, that human nature has no other ground than itself. Whatever *its* nature is, therefore, *it* originates from humanity's extraordinary capacity to imagine, create, and realize what we call historical realities. And here is what, to my mind, critical Islam borrows from the Marxist position: the assertion that these historical realities shape and *produce* specific forms of human-being (those could be forms of human slavery and fundamentalism or of human freedom and democracy, both explained via Islam) does not mean that they *create* humanity in an ontological way. Indeed, in Islam (as in other religions and cultural systems) there are numerous moments that speak of such creation but their multiplicity and historical dispersion perfectly illustrate the unconquerable groundlessness of human essence.

Autonomy versus Heteronomy

For Muslim critical thinkers, critique offers a double escape from the heteronomy of classical Islamic theology and from the heteronomy of the Enlightenment's autonomous secularist subject. *Autonomy* (of oneself or one's society), in the context of critical Islam, is constructed through critique – always acting as simultaneously self-critique and self-interrogation – and it can exist only as a project infinitely questioning itself. The achievement of *autonomy*, in the political and ethical sense of the term indeed, is possible through the poesis of the self, which constitutes itself through its own self-critique. This auto-poesis is a historical process. Critical Islam does not take a step against religion as such – the Qur'an or the Sunnah. Rather, it maintains that their emergence, legitimation, authorization, and canonical execution – in fact, their sacredness – belong to history, which makes the *arche* and the *telos* of the Islamic social imaginary determinable.

The process of external authorization (by God, Reason, or any ahistorical, i.e. *timeless* entity) is termed *heteronomy* in the book. The term, borrowed by Kant, is used to signify the kind of politics that stems from transcendental authority and goes against the multiple and multifarious worldly modes of thinking. God (at least the Islamic God) is perfect heteronomy because He is not a subject in the sense of a living being acting and knowing itself acting in the flow of time. The kind of politics that legitimizes itself via purely heteronomous frameworks of reasoning is criticized in the book because precisely this type of politics abrogates the capacity for decision by displacing decision to an unknowable and unreachable beyond (God). On the contrary, the project of a Western-Islamic public sphere, I hope, alerts to the parameters and conditions of decision via (self-)interrogation and openness to radical uncertainty. Intellectual work (which dwells in uncertainty and self-examination) requires also an openness – quite the opposite of heteronomy – which is simultaneously radically focused on the present and tremendously invested in the future.

The Notions Political *and* Public Intellectual

The practice of critique is always a matter of politics and poesis. Throughout the book I have tried to explain their intertwinement with recourse to terminology derived from Plato. I am also indebted to Davide Panagia's work on the intertwined relationship between the poetics of political thinking and democracy, and to Sheldon Wolin's insight, in *Politics and Vision*, that politics is a historical imaginative invention in a particular setting, explored across time and space on terms set by that random starting point but never confined to it.[12]

The role of the Muslim intellectual figure as related to the emergence of a particular space of questioning and debate (the Western-Islamic public sphere) is performative. In a number of passages (and especially in chapter 4) I have compared the Muslim intellectual to Plato's poet. In Book X of the *Republic* Plato argues that if poetry is a dangerous *pharmakon* (poison), one must interact with another *pharmakon* (cure, antidote) – philosophy – that would expose the real nature of poetry. To expose poetry's nature, though, means literally to produce it, to bring it to performance (the Greek term is *theasis*), to engage it in a theatrical gesture.[13] This is entirely consistent with Plato's apprehension against poetry and the poets, namely that they create myths animated by mimesis (via impersonation, performativity, and theatricality). In a paradoxical fashion, philosophy for Plato acts as the appropriate *pharmakon* and obliterates the danger of poetry by assuming the knowledge of mimesis and also by reproducing mimesis. It is not accidental that in the *Republic* philosophy is staged as myth in its ambition to overpower poetic mimesis. Plato's aim most probably is not to resolve the dispute between philosophy and poetry simply by exiling the poets from the polis but rather to show that the self-knowledge of poetry belongs, in the final instance, to philosophy. Thus, the Platonic dialogue not only preserves the poetic encounter in form but also incorporates it into the very performance of philosophy.

The quarrel between philosophy and poetry is not meant to be resolved, precisely because their intertwinement (as each other's lack) serves to conceal the main political problems of the *Republic*. And here is what, in my analysis, seems the main task of the Muslim intellectual if thought via Plato's oppositions: to demonstrate that the entire proposition that sets poetry against philosophy and thus sets society's mythographic imagination (where religion doubtlessly

belongs) against its rational-analytical propensity is a *political* enterprise at its core. Whichever way this quarrel is decided – whether
privileging one side or interweaving them somehow – is always a
political process. Moreover, the Muslim intellectual's task and
responsibility is, my argument suggests, to show the radical significance of the political itself by engaging, evaluating, and, indeed,
performing the relationship of the political to the *poetic* in the
present socio-historical moment that I define as an emergent
Western-Islamic public sphere.

This book is structured in four chapters and a conclusion. The first
chapter, called "The Politics of Critical Islam," explains the
concept, praxis, and importance of critical Islam for the emergence
of a Western-Islamic public sphere. For these Muslim critical
thinkers, critique offers a double escape from heteronomous Islamic
theology (religious fundamentalism) and from the dogmatism of the
Enlightenment's autonomous secularist subject (the Kantian
subject). Autonomy (of oneself or one's society), in the context of
critical Islam, I argue in this chapter, is constructed through the
poesis of critique – simultaneously self-critique and self-interrogation – and it can exist only as a project infinitely questioning itself.
The second chapter, "Critical Islam inside the Academia," looks at
the academic discourses of critical Islam via the examples of
Quranic hermeneutics (Muhammed Arkoun, Nasr Abu Zayd),
reformation Islamic theology (Tariq Ramadan), anthropology
(Malek Chebel), and psychoanalysis (Fethi Benslama). My main
concern here is to show the diversity of approaches to Islamic religious dogma and to expose the variety of faces, sometimes
contradictory and exclusive, of critical Islam's scholastic strategies
for the relativization of a rigorous fundamentalist religious message.
In the third chapter, called "The Western-Islamic Public Sphere in
the Light of the North American Post-Colonial Studies and the
European Polemics against Islam," I show how two debates on critical Islam – one American and one European – question the
legitimacy of critical Islam, reducing its practice and commitments
either to the new imperial rhetoric of orientalism (Saba Mahmood)
or to religious fundamentalism camouflaged in liberal rhetoric
(Pascal Bruckner). As a response to this debate, I suggest that the
Western-Islamic public sphere offers a third view arising from crit-

ical Islam's commitment to intellectual work as a portal to the open horizons of history. In the final, fourth, and longest chapter, called "Critical Islam and the Politics of Literary Texts," I look at the work of four exemplary Western-Islamic literary figures – Abdelwahab Meddeb, Ali Eteraz, Nadeem Aslam, and Orhan Pamuk – all whom I find crucial to the emergence of a Western-Islamic public sphere. The desire to finish with a commentary of literary texts is motivated by a conviction deployed throughout the book that literature's unique relationship to knowledge and critique is essentially political: this is based on the understanding that the literary always pertains to the domains of the social, the historical, and the worldly, and thus, by the virtue of its mere existence disputes the ahistorical claims of any heteronomy. Moreover, the interrogation of the poetical elements of a text is also an attempt to understand what determines the parameters of social poesis itself. Precisely for this reason, the analysis through the lenses of the Western-Islamic public sphere goes beyond the disciplinary confines of aesthetic theory or literary criticism and it is a political and culturological analysis in essence: it seeks to determine and describe the main performative moments in the social imagination involved in the Western-Islamic encounter.

Methodologically, the book is built upon a combination of different types of integrative analysis: from subtle navigation through a number of theoretical frameworks and debates in the humanities and social sciences (including the classical philosophical concepts of *autonomy* and *heteronomy*, and debates on critique, post-coloniality, religion, and secularism), and Islamic studies (debates on religious hermeneutics, dogmatic theology, and Quranic studies), to critical exegetic readings of primary sources written in French and Arabic, and from political discourse analysis to cultur-ological reflection on the foundations, assumptions, and ethical commitments of the analyzed intellectual production.

Finally, the most significant contribution of the book is the intro-duction and elaboration of a new concept – the Western-Islamic public sphere – currently non-existent in the theorizations on reli-gion and the public sphere. Only a nuanced, informed, and attentive approach to the complexities of the textual and political practices that involve religion could generate conceptually new tools that would transcend the atemporal, rigid, and heteronomous dogmata of any religious or secularist project. The Western-Islamic public sphere is designed as an engagement with, and an alternative response to, precisely those aspects of religion and public power that tend to employ heteronomous frameworks in defense of their perpetuity. In a sense, the Western-Islamic public sphere is a prism through which the transcendentalist discourses (regardless of whether religious or secularist) of literalism, exclusion, and dogma should be exposed and overcome.

1

The Politics of Critical Islam

The Praxis of Critique

The term critique has a complicated history. It derives simultaneously from the Greek *krino*, which means, in Reinhart Koselleck's
translation, "to cut," "to select," "to decide," "to judge," "to fight,"
"to measure," and "to quarrel"[1] and the Greek *krisis*, which, in
Stathis Gourgouris's translation, means "the decision to pronounce
difference or even the decision to differ, to dispute."[2] Both etymolo-
gies suggest that the term, being productive of meanings and
derivates, is nonetheless related to the political as a register of non-
neutral judgments. Decisions in the Greek polis are based on
judgments for which someone – those who pronounce the judgment
– takes responsibility. The subject, unthinkable outside the Greek
polis, is naturally involved in the political through critical interrogation. Moreover, since the subject differs and differentiates at the
same time, the semantic scope of the term – as Gourgouris insists –
naturally includes self-critique because suspicion cannot be limited
only to the objective world. Therefore, the gesture of critique is
authentic and political only if it is predicated on infinite self-reflex-
ivity and self-critique.

The term "critical Islam" is a theoretical construct invented to
reflect a critical mode of analysis generated by the intelligentsia of
the Muslim Diaspora in the West and does not claim theological
accuracy. More precisely, critical Islam is an analytic approach to
religion that promotes critical reading of the original Islamic text
(the Qur'an) and traditions (the hadiths) in order to open from
within new meaningful horizons for the religious message. This
gesture is not only a fundamental break from – and a highly suspicious one to – the classical theology of Islam, because it involves
de-sacralization of the divine but also, it is political in this classical
Greek sense because it is loaded with internal self-reflexive critique.

Islam is to be secured – *saved* from the inaccessible dogmatic language of the religious tradition – through the relentless critique of religion itself. This is not just a deliberate attempt to think with Islam against the excess of Islam in order the access to some more authentic Islam to be opened, but a political act – constitutive of a public sphere – as long as it critically targets dogmatic theology (the heteronomous framework of Islam when thought sufficient for the generation of political order here on Earth) and the social when predicated on rationalist and secularist assumptions of autonomy. Therefore, critical Islam is an engagement with the social reality and, as my argument suggests, it is a peculiar Western-Islamic phenomenon, politically oriented towards the West, an engagement that positions the Islamic religion first in history (it subjects Islam to secularization) and then within a Western cultural-historical framework.

Yet, with respect to critical Islam, the most important questions remain connected to the lures of the timeless frameworks of heteronomy (God) and autonomy (the humanist subject). After all, the whole classical Islamic theology is centered around this famous hadith narrated by Al-Ghazali: "The man who explains the Qur'an according to his personal opinion shall take his place in Hell."[3] Is the rise of the subject possible in the faith-based context of total submission (this is precisely the original meaning of the Arabic word Islam) to the Absolute Other? And, then, if the subject is possible and critical Islam is a particular religious affirmation of subjectivity, how does critical Islam prevent the reduction of religious mythos to a set of mythologies devoid of divine meaning? Classical Islam channels a particular obsessive worship of the absolute heteronomous, the transcendent, the One and the Only God. How is an engagement possible 'not with god but with God' who is radical alterity and who requires radical incapacitation of the subject, rather than cognition and communication?

It should be noted that despite the fact that critical Islam historicizes and de-transcendentalizes the absolute alterity of Allah, it does not adopt the Kantian notion of a pure autonomous and rationalistic mind. The pure autonomy, in that context, is no less metaphysical than the heteronomy of Allah. Self-referential and tautological, the Cartesian–Kantian idea of autonomy (*I think therefore I am,* or *I am that I am,* I is a being-in-itself) is a theological concept because it posits itself as an absolute existing outside history. It knows history because it knows itself but it cannot know anything outside itself. In that regard, the classical Enlightenment notion of autonomy that comes through reason cannot admit or enter in a relationship with alterity because it is itself heteronomous in a universe of meanings where the authority of all other absolutes is, by definition, undermined.[4] Within the Kantian framework transcendence is internalized through the creation of a heteronomous moral subject who becomes the measure of all things. The problem is that secularist reasoning in the general Kantian scheme does not just shift the emphasis from the agency of the divine to the agency of the human subject, but, rather, it transcendentalizes the subject, putting it in God's place. Reason, however, is not necessarily inherently theological or metaphysical but it becomes such only when it is put in the transcendental architectural framework of religion.

At the same time, critical Islam is a highly contested field of intellectual engagement because it requires, at least as far as the work of Muslim intellectuals discussed in the book is concerned – Muhammad Arkoun, Nasr Abu Zayd, Abdelwahab Meddeb, Tariq Ramadan, Malek Chebel, Fethi Benslama, Nadeem Aslam, Ali Eteraz, Orhan Pamuk, among others, the double work of knowing the canon of Islam (or the tradition) and the modes of interrogating it. It has to be noted that the critical work of Muslim intellectuals rooted in interdisciplinary inquiry – hermeneutics, theology, history, literature, anthropology, psychoanalysis – is first of all self-critical and disciplinary. This means that the normative logic of the Islamic canon(s) is taken to its limit precisely in order to interrogate the construction of this limit. Critical Islam is, therefore, a transformation of this construction or a deconstruction as long as what remains after the deconstruction is never reducible to the canon. Deconstruction of Islamic theology does not mean annihilation of theology but it does not enable its repetition either. This, in essence, is the *political* and *poetical* substance of critical Islam.

Examples of Religious Heteronomies

In 2005, the gigantic and highly popular Islamic (Arabic and English) information portal, onislam.net, published, after a public inquiry in the youth section, a fatwa by a famous professor of *fiqh* (Arab. Islamic jurisprudence) at the University of Jerusalem. The fatwa issued by Dr. Hisam al-Din Ibn Musa Afaneh explores flogging for educational purposes.[5] The scholar elaborates the issue in several points: a teacher is prohibited from beating his student solely on the basis of disagreement or out of anger, but following what the Prophet Muhammad has said, he is allowed to use violence in cases when all other measures have failed. Moreover, a student is to be urged into prayer when he is seven and beaten into it at the age of ten. As a diligent scholar, Hisam al-Din Ibn Musa Afaneh also mentions that there exists a discussion among the *ulema* (Arab. religious scholars) on the number of lashes to be inflicted upon a student (between three and ten according to different authoritative hadith narrators: Bukhari, Muslim, Abu Dawuud, and Al-Tirmidhi). Finally, the mufti concludes that the abolishment of violence as an educational means would have a negative impact on the Islamic educational process and it would ultimately betray the continuity of the Islamic tradition.

If one looks at the comprehensive Muslim tradition and its most authoritative sources, there is seemingly enough evidence to support the application of violence in different cases. The fatwa issued in 2005 is surprisingly similar to a centuries-old reflection by Ibn Taymiyya (d. 1328) in his comprehensive collection of Hanbalite authoritative fatwas. There, the medieval Muslim jurist and philosopher comments briefly on the corruption of children by their teachers. A proper pedagogical practice associated with severe punishments, Ibn Taymiyya maintains, is strictly related to a divine imperative requiring children to be taught and raised in obedience to God and His Prophet. Taymiyya reminds, and this is repeated in the 2005 fatwa, that a child has to be taught ritual prayer at five and beaten into it when he is ten.[6]

Certainly the history of the category of punishment in the legal-theological Muslim imagination is too complex to be exhausted with several examples that, all the more, run the risk of reifying misrepresentations of Islam. It is well known by scholars in Islamic theology that there exists a distinction when the term beating is employed regarding general situations and when related to legal punishment.[7] Obviously the beating of students for educational purposes falls into the general use of the term, and, also, the historical contexts of the two fatwas are quite different. Yet, violence sneaks through other authoritative doors. The famous, controversial, and often debated verse 4:34 from the Qur'an at first glance advocates violence over women: "Men have authority over women because God has made one superior over the other, and because they spend their wealth to maintain them. Good women are obedient. They guard their unseen parts because God has guarded them. As for those from whom you fear disobedience, admonish them and send them to beds apart and beat them. Then, if they obey you, take no further action against them. Surely God is high, supreme."[8]

In addition to this Quranic prescription, there are hundreds of hadiths that circulate in the English-Arabic public sphere and that have been taken for authentic and authoritative. They are usually quoted by legal and theological figures today (with or without training in Islamic theology) who advocate in fashion or language (scandalous, from our present day perspective) violent behaviour in support the divine or the prophetic authority. Among the numerous examples, I have chosen several: Anas bin Malik (d. 709) reports that the Prophet said "No human may prostrate to another, and if it were permissible I would have ordered a wife to prostrate to her husband because of the enormity of his rights over her. By God, if there is an ulcer excreting puss from his feet to the top of his head, and she licked it for him she would not fulfill his rights."[9] This hadith was the precise reason the African-American Muslim basketball player Abdul Rauf in 1996 refused to stand while the American national anthem was playing during basketball games. The act of "prostrating," he argued, was offensive to Muslim sensibilities because it is un-Islamic to salute a national flag or stand to a national anthem.[10]

Another hadith attributed to the Prophet proclaims, "A woman comes in the image of a devil and leaves in the image of a devil."[11] According to Abou El-Fadl, a professor in Islamic law at UCLA, the rest of the narration says that if a man is aroused by a foreign woman, he should satisfy his desire lawfully with his own wife. Perhaps not surprisingly there is a whole cluster of hadiths that discusses the fate of women in hellfire. Again Abou El-Fadl gives a comprehensive account of those traditions and their different versions according to the narrators. Ibn Abbas, one of the Prophet's companions, has been reported to have said that a woman has two covers of modesty, marriage and the grave.[12] Probably this is the reason why Abu Hamid al-Ghazali, relying on those traditions, suggests that a married woman has to be confined in "the inner sanctum of her house"; she should not leave her house without permission or talk to the neighbours. If she does leave her home, she should stick to the least crowded spaces, she should not speak to anyone, mostly she should occupy herself with pleasing her husband, and she should not aim to play any public role.[13] Effectively, the grave becomes a metaphor for the modest life that a pious married woman should live. What those traditions do – whether narrated by strong chains of transmission or fabricated (which in itself is a serious theological inquiry) – is to project a grave-like existence for women on Earth based only on the notion that probably the Prophet himself, guided by the Divine Will, would approve of it. Nadeem Aslam's semi-autobiographical novel *Maps for Lost Lovers* engages exactly these traditions that inform and put into divine perspective the actions of the pious in the Muslim community.[14]

The highly popular *tafsir* (Arab. exegetical commentary of the Qur'an) of the medieval Muslim exegete and theologian Al-Tabari (d. 923) fits well in the interpretative framework of divinely sanctioned violence. In his commentary of the 4:34 verse, al-Tabari maintains that the application of physical violence for punishment of women should be understood within the divine framework of obedience of the wife before her husband, whose most important duty, on the other hand, is total submission to Allah. Commenting on the controversial verse, al-Tabari maintains: "if they [women] refuse to reverse to what has been their duty to you [men], then keep them tight in their houses, and then beat them in order to make them return to their duty (*wājib*) to obey Allah in what has been mandated to them further to your rights. And the exegetes have said that the characteristic of the beating permitted by Allah to the husband of the rebellious [one] to beat her, is that it is not severe."[15]

All of these examples, deliberately chosen to shock and to provoke, could be countered with numerous other examples from the Qur'an and the Sunnah that speak to tendencies quite opposite to those described above. For example, there are available reports that reveal the Prophet Muhammad treated his wives with care and respect. Those reports make it evident that he was not a dictator inside his family, which, in turn, probably means that it is highly unlikely that the Prophet truly pronounced the misogynist sayings quoted above.[16] Even from a theological perspective, it is unlikely to think that the sacred Quranic scripture would elevate to a semi-divine status the male human being in general, and the Prophet Muhammad in particular, and recommend the female to be once and forever a humble servant of the male. This is also inconsistent with the overall logic of the Qur'an, in which it is stated that "none can know the soldiers of God except God."[17] Even though this verse

THE POLITICS OF CRITICAL ISLAM

talks about the nineteen angels that guard hell and seems to say that only God knows why those angels are nineteen and not a different number, it is also a magnificent representation of the radical transcendentalism of Islam and its concept of God: everyone can aspire to be a soldier of God and perform the impossible to achieve this status, but only God knows His soldiers. Everyone is allowed access to God's benevolence but no one is guaranteed a secure entrance there.

Against Heteronomy

Therefore, the question of what comprises the authoritarian voice or interpretation of Islam – to which hopefully critical Islam provides a reflective-critical response – is extremely important to the discussion of all theology and praxis of Islam. Namely, pertinent to the discussion of whether those partial, violent, and sometimes fabricated traditions – which in all cases are products of specific historical circumstances – should be literally translated, followed, and diligently obeyed by Muslims today, even if they are highly recommended by unquestionable religious authorities.

It is true that all authority in Islam stems from the sacred Islamic scripture, the Qur'an, the hadith texts (the narratives of the life, deeds, and silences of the Prophet Muhammad), the *tafsir* (the exegetical commentaries of the hadiths), the judicial tractates followed by educational texts, philosophical works, and classic literary pieces. All of these texts comprise the theologically, ethically, and legally normative Islamic framework and they ensure the continuity of the Islamic tradition.[18] However, it is also true that the Islamic tradition, based on texts and practices, is a result of controversial and cumulative efforts at interpretation and transmission that are first and foremost *human* and *historical*, which is also another way to say *secular*. Simply put, the Qur'an and the *Sunnah* (the hadith corpus) that just speak by themselves, without historical contexts and people in them, do not exist. A tradition is always constructed even when it invokes the sacred and immutable text of the Qur'an or the seemingly reliable narratives of the Sunnah. And precisely the claim about the constructedness of the tradition is crucial to critical Islam. At a more abstract level, the non-historical understanding of the Islamic tradition conceals a trend that is destroying the legacy of another very rich Islam, banning, for example, books such as *A Thousand and One Nights* and the poetry of Abu Nuwas (d. 814), which have been transmitted in Muslim civilization for centuries[19] and which continue to inspire much of the artistic endeavours of what I call critical Islam today.

Yet, the choice between a critical historical reading of Islam and dogmatic theology is theoretically complex and even more difficult to resolve in the actual praxis of the Islamic religion. Ebrahim Moosa, for example, suggests that there is a certain level at which one could speak about multiple Islams, today and in history.[20] This proposition refers to the multiple discursive traditions through which Muslims imagine themselves, and to the embodiments of these traditions in various, orthodox and heterodox, enormously varied and highly contested, Islamic practices. Yet having admitted this multiplicity as a pragmatic reality, Moosa quickly changes the terms of the discussion, insisting that the debate over whether Islam is one or is multiple is fruitless because, even if being intuitively true, the proposition that Islam is multiple and dispersed does not appeal to the collective Muslim sensibility.[21] This, I take, as a particularly illuminating remark, made by a prominent secular Muslim intellectual and a professor of Islam in the United States, about the predicaments that critical Islam has to resolve and publicly announce, mostly regarding its own standing in the contemporary Islamic intellectual landscape, on a theoretical and pragmatic level.

In terms of the orthodox Islamic theology (which is also the strongest of all Islamic commitments and a common denominator for the "collective Islamic sensibility" because it is first and foremost a metaphysical claim about God and therefore is considered immutable), it is common knowledge that the entrenched practices and beliefs associated with the Qur'an and the hadiths should be regarded as something given once and for all with the revelation and the life of the Prophet, existing in smooth continuity throughout sacred Islamic history and, moreover, as something which should be replicated across Muslim societies and throughout the centuries. Needless to say, this approach eliminates the complex history of the whole Islamic civilization because it ignores from the very beginning the possibility for any social-imaginary constitution of Islam. Muslims, according to this perspective, reside in the sacred Islamic eschaton where their whole profane being is generated by an elsewhere and is lived as an elsewhere; worldly life simply moves from birth to death to salvation where the last term signifies the beginning of the true life, the life of transcendental security and eternity.

In this scenario, the subject resigns itself to its sacred fate, precisely as the etymological meaning of the word Islam suggests. God founds the immanent, evanescent, and temporal world but He does not participate in it (in order to keep His transcendence) and thus remains inimitable in the exercise of divine authority. All human authority, in comparison to the divine authority, by definition becomes contradictory. The community of the elect believers does not own any of its proper anthropological characteristics because its existence is fully conditioned by the prophetic history: "He it is who hath placed you as viceroys of the earth and hath exalted some of you in rank above others, that He may try you by (the test of) that which He hath given you. Lo! Thy Lord is swift in prosecution, and lo! He is Forgiving, Merciful."[22] And also "Lo! Allah is the knower of the Unseen of the heavens and the earth. Lo! He is Aware of the secret of (men's) breasts. He it is who hath made you regents in the earth; so he who disbelieveth, his disbelief be on his own head. Their disbelief increaseth for the disbelievers, in their Lord's sight, naught save abhorrence. Their disbelief increaseth for the disbelievers naught save loss."[23] It is obvious that in the Quranic scheme the One and Only God is not only the Unknown and the One who reigns in absolute singularity but also the One who commands – from His heteronomous position of transcendence – all social conditions.[24]

One of the most important distinctions, therefore, between a strictly dogmatic reading of Islam and a critical engagement with the Islamic tradition is related to the conceptualization of creation. A dogmatic reading sees creation as a strictly theological event in which God created the universe and withdrew from in it in order to preserve His absolute heteronomy. Nonetheless, this absolutely transcendent God needs the temporary world precisely because in it His power ruptures and somehow from the outside dictates the parameters of any historical event, of any worldliness, which is traceable, feasible, and defined by spatial and temporal characteristics. This, indeed, is the magnificent demiurgic power of the divine to create the world *ex nihilo* and to control its movement and direction. However, the world understood as created and controlled by an omnipotent, omniscient, and ubiquitous external force is hardly left with any space for human agency and politics.

The secular power of poesis, on the other hand, which is inherent in the framework of critical Islam, confronts the notion of the almighty, all knowing, and perfect demiourgos. Creation *ex nihilo* in this secular line of thinking actually signifies the capacity of humanity to imagine the world, to imagine things that do not exist in the world, and to perform on that basis (to its own benefit or destruction) outside of any external frame of reference or guarantee. This is precisely the capacity of humanity to act autonomously and politically in the world and as the world, inasmuch as acting politically means to decide on the conditions of life independently of any authority that requires obedient submission. God is undoubtedly an important signification in the history of all human societies inasmuch as his existence, power, and importance are a magnificent representation of humanity's autonomous capacity to imagine a heteronomous authority and to submit to it (or rebel against it for that matter). The phenomenon of voluntary submission is understood here entirely in historical terms, namely as a worldly product of a worldly force. Even when it comes to moments of radical alteration that change the existing historical parameters and for which transcendentalist explanations seem plausible, they are seen, as this overused phrase suggests, as the *cunning* of history. History can produce moments of discontinuity that are not recognizable in previous historical patterns, moments that seem to come out of nothing and mean nothing but nonetheless are not theological in essence.[25] Critical Islam, therefore, approaches dogmatic theology as a text (one among many religious texts) and aims to subvert the framework of engagement with dogma from pious submission to active commitment, where the latter suggests the intellectual work of constant interrogation and (self-) critique.

A critical analysis of Islam, therefore, is encountered on the one hand with a body of texts both solid and resistant to critical re-readings, with their established, authoritative, and sometimes immutable interpretations, and, on the other hand, with a universe of Islamic practices trying to engage the Islamic transcendentalist discourses in various performative languages. The fatwa examples, some Quranic passages, and some of the most frequently cited hadiths and tafsirs quoted above, as well as the desire that their original message be transmitted and replicated in social practice, even today in certain Muslim communities, is testimony that those texts speak to a tradition that is both important and alive. Namely, this is the tradition that venerates in a literalist and strict way the divine creation and submits all human action to it. My argument, following the argument of critical Islam, is simple: even the transcendence of God is historically embedded. Theory and praxis, the transcendent and the immanent, for that matter, are closely related here because they condition and produce each other in every moment when the tradition is evoked in defense of a certain practice.

Only a critical rereading of the dogmatic tradition, however, and rendering it vulnerable/accessible to modification and change can prevent mindless idolization. The problem that mainly preoccupies critical Islam, therefore, is not the distinction per se of the transcendent and the immanent dimensions of Islam (and critical Islam does not advocate the immanent over the transcendent) but rather the historical instances of their closure as self-sufficient horizons in and of themselves. In that case, any immanent practice – that is executed or followed only because it is seen as divinely sanctioned – necessarily becomes transcendent because it involves by default a submission to the authority of the Other. This does not mean that for critical Islam the absolute and unknowable Allah, as the most potent symbol in the Islamic imaginary, does not possess authority, but rather that His authority cannot have an a priori objective value against which all human things or actions should be measured.

Theory and Praxis

The Western-Islamic public sphere is designed as a fragmented and ethical engagement that acquires theoretical density through its relationship to history. The Western-Islamic public sphere appears at the intersection of the micro and the macro modalities of the historical. The concept of a Western-Islamic public sphere is supposed to historicize the absolute, metaphysical, and timeless frameworks of both Islam and the West through the exploration of their dynamic relationship with another historical category, namely the *secular.* Otherwise, the terms Islam and the West should not be employed in other than rhetorical fashion. At the same time, since the Greek polis, the public sphere has been a space above and beyond the individual. It is a quintessential expression of the political order, which, because of its relational duty – to secure the circumstances under which people live in common – acts upon the force of affect. As long as the public sphere presupposes relationship with the other, it requires affective tropes – solidarity, fraternity, and commonality – to preserve the contact. Since the time of the Greek polis, it has not mattered whether the public domain is organized around the dialogue of the agora (the polis), the divine scheme (theocracy), the revolutionary constitution (republic), the bill of rights (democracy), the welfare state (liberalism), the charismatic leader (totalitarianism), or the communal rights (multiculturalism); its existence has been legitimized through narratives that belong to the timeless register of heteronomy. The community, the individual, or God act as transcendent, highly normative references that provide with identity any political existence. Therefore, the public space embodies the aporia of community (as long as community is always based on this affective normative relation) whose stake is, in the end, the monopoly of whichever grand-narrative currently enjoys the most public currency.

The Western-Islamic public sphere is thinkable through the secular as an open and infinite process of de-transcendentalization, i.e. of transforming the metaphysical into discursive reality. As long as both religion and secularism claim to be the universal and absolute orders of the world, and not to comply with any historical reality, they can be approached as transcendental metaphysical projects. Though conscious of the distinctions between the metaphysics of Islam and the metaphysics of secularism, here I am interested not as much in exploring them or equating them as in the elaboration of the notion of the Western-Islamic public sphere as one possible perspective for overcoming their dialectical relationship.

If secularism, with its adjacent concept of civil religion, is impossible because it either results in republican celebrations or in fascism (the law is God), and theocracy (God is law) is impossible because it establishes the kingdom of God on Earth (the caliphate) and deprives the communal and the individual of their agencies – secularism and theocracy are therefore ideologies – then the whole relationship between religion and state, which by default is based on affect, should be rethought.[26] The Western-Islamic public sphere is a space of *autonomy*, a discursive space coming out of the resistance to *heteronomy*.[27] The Western-Islamic public sphere forms a process rather than a substance because inside it any singular truth is exposed to other singular truths in discursive relationship, which, beyond being only affectual and resistant, is historical. In that regard, the Western-Islamic public sphere is secular (imbricated in history-in-the-making) and not secularist; it is Islamic rather than Islamist. Finally, the Western-Islamic public sphere is conceived as a horizon of hope for both reason and religion – neither of them is lost. Precisely when they are thought as intertwined and juxtaposed

THE POLITICS OF CRITICAL ISLAM

– in being-in-common – in their worldly, time-bound, and historical imbrication, religion and reason are *protected* from becoming
impenetrable unities.

The Meaning of Critique

Critical Islam, which is also the basic agent of the Western-Islamic
public sphere, should not be taken, though, for a rigorous and systematic theory. Neither should it be seen as a magical panacea for
all problems related to dogmatism in the universe of Islam or religion in general. This does not mean, however, that critical Islam
cannot engage in theoretical problems or, indeed, produce theories
(it does produce theories in the domain of Quranic hermeneutics
as the work of Muhammad Arkoun and Nasr Abou Zayd has
shown or as the work of Fethi Benslama, for example, reveals in
the domain of psychoanalysis of religion).[28] The reason why critical Islam cannot be theoretically defined is certainly related to the
fact that it originates in different disciplines – it could be
hermeneutic, psychoanalytic, journalistic, or literary inquiry at the
same time. Mainly, however, it cannot be theoretically defined due
to its secular and critical components. As a practice of critique,
neither critical Islam nor the intellectual universe that it presupposes – the Western-Islamic public sphere – can be restricted to/by
an external set of rules for what would be critical, Western, or
Islamic about it because a strict definition would defeat the intelli-
gence of the practice on all grounds. Whatever the boundaries of
the notions "critical," "Western," and "Islamic," they are themselves subject to constant re-examination because critique is not a
theory but a practice that is at once poetic, experimental, and sceptical (and for that matter political) towards all kinds of
heteronomous thinking.

It is ironic in many ways that Edward Said's main contribution
to critical theory is his dedication to "worldliness," which refers to
the public intellectual's relevance to society as well as to the embed-
dedness of texts in their particular worlds. It is ironic because the
Orientalism era inspired a scholarship that tends to read the text as
an unconditional defense of the religious practice of Islam against
all forms of secular thinking, which, especially in radical postcolonial and anti-imperialist circles, are regarded as related to
imperialism and Christianity.[29] *The World, the Text and the Critic* is

actually Said's most passionate defense of secular scholarship as opposed to a religious one:

> The point is that texts have ways of existing that even in their most rarefied forms are always enmeshed in circumstance, time, place and society – hence, they are in the world and hence worldly. Whether the text is preserved or put aside for a period, whether it is on a library shelf or not: these matters have to do with a text's being in the world, which is a more complicated matter than the private process of reading. The same implications are undoubtedly true of critics in their capacities as readers and writers in the world.[30]

Said's argument is that religious criticism (criticism that uncritically advocates the dogma) serves the status quo; it essentializes, eternalizes, and unifies cultural or socio-political formations as opposed to secular criticism which is "non-coercive," "life-enhancing," and destined to cultivate new forms of existence.[31] Even though Edward Said has never strictly defined the term "secular criticism," in *The World, the Text and the Critic* he provides an elaborate description of a task that may include theoretical work but mostly is related to practices of thinking and writing. In terms of the knowledge that it mobilizes, this task is quintessentially literary (in the sense of imaginative), a fact that is usually undermined in contemporary discussions of secularism.

The discussion of the terrain of the secular is important for the model of a Western-Islamic public sphere precisely because there exists a scholarly tendency that, as mentioned, ironically goes back to Said's seminal work *Orientalism*, and that equates intellectually and even historically the theological and the secular. The Western-Islamic public sphere is a critical project hinging on the distinction between the secular and the theological (in the sense of dogmatic) and if the distinction is not well understood then the politics of this critical intellectual endeavour may remain miscomprehended.

In a 2008 article called "Historical Notes on the Idea of Secular Criticism," Talal Asad makes an attempt to stabilize the notion of secular criticism against Said's earlier arguments in *The World, the Text and the Critic*. He provides a genealogy of the Greek term *krisis* (which, as mentioned, is at the root of the notion of critique), accurately insisting that the unquestionable link between critique and universal reason is entirely the work of European modernity. Asad also mentions the relation between *krisis* and *parrhesia*, which he translates via Foucault as "fearless speech."[32] At the same time, not even paying enough attention to Foucault's own historical framework in the 1978 text "What is Critique?," Asad undermines the notion of *parrhesia* by connecting it to Christian confessional practices and, later on, to the Kantian rationalist-transcendentalist ethics. Therefore, he concludes, the concept of fearless speech is actually derived from a Christian understanding of service to truth, which has entered the historical imaginary of Kantianism, where, as it is well known, the critical faculty is always predicated on a priori structures of truth. In this scheme, which defines much of Western Enlightenment thought, the freedom of speech is always measured against the standard of an external and universal truth. Therefore, there is indeed no such thing as free speech, because any freedom that comes with it has to be subject in advance to the measurable, calculable, and always external principles of the scientific laboratory. From here the final argument is easy to discern: secular criticism (the Saidian term) is an inherently metaphysical notion – because it always obeys an external set of rules – that could be easily recognized in the institutional structures of secularism, and, for that matter, it is structurally the same as theology. So, the secular is a condition for the emergence of a new Enlightenment theology (which is, in fact, a de-secularized version of Christianity) called secularism, which is, in essence, a re-articulation of religion in modernity. Therefore, for a great number of theorists (not only for Talal Asad), the whole question of secularization is essentially deceptive. Christianity performs a trick by which it erases itself from the field of religion (via Enlightenment and secularization) in order to establish the rules of religion for all other religions in the world.

There is an unquestionable historical validity to Talal Asad's argument (which is actually a concise repetition of the much more complexly elaborated philosophical-historical argument of Charles Taylor in the magnum opus *A Secular Age*[33]) but it still misses the main question, which I hope the reflection on the Western-Islamic public sphere raises from a different angle: is it possible to talk about critique or fearless free speech (*parrhesia*) at all when the origin of truth is not itself deconstructed, i.e. subject to radical interrogation?[34] Even if critique or free speech is tied to a particular regime of truth, it is still something different from this regime and it cannot and should not be reduced to any kind of Christian or Kantian ethics. If critique is going to deserve its name and if it is going to generate social projects, it cannot be subservient to any external truth or to anything in general. It has to be placed outside the master-servant structure of relations, and, in a sense, it has to behave as an anarchic mechanism.[35] This understanding of critique goes well beyond the scientific exegetical apparatus that Enlightenment rationalism requires and that measures the meaning of any object against a rigorous scientist or technologist standard of truth. Asad is certainly right, following the well-known Weberian argument, to insist that precisely much of the textual hermeneutics of Protestantism aligns itself with the rationalism of the West in order to produce a major secularizing apparatus but the fact that secularism is a particular institutional regime of truth does not necessarily mean that the *secular* itself – as a category related to time, history, and, indeed, critique – is bound to obey, in every historical instance, the institutional metaphysics of secularism.

And while it is true that critique is always possible as a historical fact – which means as a specific worldly (and often) polemical practice – it is certainly limiting to understand its stakes as subject to the logic of the scientific laboratory. Such reading of the Enlightenment's legacy is also impoverished because it aims to reduce the Enlightenment's impact only to the rationalist, scientist, and technologist regimes of calculation, assuming that precisely their mechanisms of reasoning dictate the tropes of all forms of intellectual critique, turning it into some kind of measurable professional knowledge. Interestingly enough, Talal Asad's analysis of the Enlightenment project coincides to a large extent with Pope Benedict's understanding of the Enlightenment (during his famous exchange with Habermas) as an entirely scientific project, which cannot offer ethical answers to the existence and purpose of man.[36] Contrary to this understanding, the Western-Islamic public sphere takes as a point of departure the praxis of critique as a sceptical and even tragic affair that challenges submission. Critical thinking, which is always political thinking inasmuch as it is engaged with the conditions of the world, dwells in the uncertainty and precariousness of history. Critical thinking does not obey any external process of authorization. As a poetic and imaginative process, critical thinking does not aspire to affirm unalterable and uncontestable truths, and it does not impose certainty in the dogmatically religious, Cartesian or Kantian sense, but rather it participates in the (trans)formation of the world via the inherently anarchic principles of interrogation and imagination.

At this point, for example, there is enough historical evidence to support the claim that the imaginative dimensions of critique contribute to the formation of the classical Western public spheres. The literary production of the late eighteenth and early nineteenth centuries turned out to be formative for modern public communication. The imaginary public, as the arguments of Benedict Anderson[37] and Jürgen Habermas[38] go, participates symbolically in the construction of the actual national audience. In the eighteenth and nineteenth centuries, the communication between civil subjects, regardless of any state hierarchies, started at the French aristocratic salons when bourgeois men of letters like Diderot and Rousseau were invited as arbiters of good taste; this type of communication was proliferated in the German literary and scientific societies, in the British tea and coffee clubs meeting for the discussion of popular novels – to multiply a few decades later in the literary supplements of mass newspapers, and in the growing network of libraries, publishing houses and literary magazines. The modern epoch is, among other things, one of access: it rejects the notion of closed communication, esoteric knowledge, or legitimated uses of reason that are designed for a select minority only. The public sphere historically comes into existence in the West when the universal reading humanity (to use the language of the Enlightenment) and the separate reading individual are mediated by a specific historical phenomenon, notably that of the nation, of the imagined community of equal individuals related into an organic community. The public sphere, therefore, responds to a new form of institutionalized imagination, which allows the individual to experience him/herself related to other individuals whom he/she has not seen, does not know, and will probably never know.

Whatever the actual shortcomings and failures of this historical model of the public sphere might be – and they have already been extensively discussed in the scholarly literature from various perspectives: feminist, postmodern, colonial, anti-humanist, sociological, and from the standpoint of the national histories of the Western states, etc. – there is a fundamental principle of intellectual production, of imaginative, creative, and critical work involved here, which encounters and transcends the stable ideologies of the closed elites at the time and contributes significantly to the new collective imaginary, namely that of the nation state. That xenophobic nationalism historically turned out to be another dangerous identity mechanism does not lessen the significance of Diderot's and

Rousseau's intellectual work, nor does it make eighteenth- and nineteenth-century literature always implicit in the darkest corners of the Enlightenment, namely the xenophobic national ideologies and imperialism. There is indeed a tragic dimension to critique and imagination (as numerous historical examples convey) because, being inseparable from the worldly contexts to which they respond and being incapable of liberating the world from its insecurities, critique and imagination betray their original task: they can work either to humanity's emancipation or to its destruction.[39]

So, the Western-Islamic public sphere, as entirely predicated on the praxis of sceptical, imaginative, political (self-)critique, evident in the academic work, public discourses, literary production, journalistic, and creative endeavors of Western Muslim intellectuals, is not immune to the danger of falling victim to nefarious ideologies. What makes me nonetheless insist on its relevance as an analytic category for the present-day state of affairs between Islam and the West is my feeling that, if taken seriously, the Western-Islamic public sphere might actually point to an emergent historical terrain that could be easily ignored if one stays locked inside the analytic vocabulary of orientalism and the various "post"-somethings: post-secular, post-modern, post-political, etc. What if the Western-Islamic public sphere is a genuine effort to think differently about the divisions between the West and Islam and the problems that demarcate their assumed identities through the category of the *secular* – where critique, imagination, politics, and intellectual work naturally belong – rather than through ambiguous significations such as the post-secular (which assumes that the secular has somehow finished: by being abolished by another, ambiguously theological, project or by having entirely completed its mission; both suggestions are untrue because of the secular's historical, inexhaustible, nature), for example? What if the post-secular designation points to our inability to engage with the secular precisely because we tend to ignore the potential of the latter for critically re-imagining the social-historical world?[40]

Finally, the Western-Islamic public sphere is an inherently democratic project that celebrates the creative and critical participation of the individual in the social world. As Hannah Arendt suggests in her seminal analysis of totalitarianism,[41] there cannot be democracy without the involvement of creative, sensitive, and imaginative people, broadly speaking, intellectuals. In fact one of the basic foundations of freedom is a culture based on rich and highly creative mechanisms, an antidote to all kinds of heteronomous ideologies, and if it disappears – as it has happened historically with the various kinds of totalitarianisms in the twentieth century (Hitler, Stalin, Mao Tse-tung, religious fundamentalism) and, more or less, with the Western culture of spectacle – then freedom disappears. The work of the critical Muslim intellectuals is important, and non-conformist precisely in that sense, because it tells us that there is something tremendously beautiful in the world of Islam and simultaneously deeply wrong in a dogmatic universe guided solely by submission to the divine. Moreover, the intellectuals – the people of critical spirit and culture – have been historically the most sensitive to all kinds of injustices: they were the first to tell that slavery was something unjust and it had to be ended; that racism and colonialism were unfair systems and they had to be abolished. The intellectuals work against the forces of instrumental rationality and calculation, striving to establish a democratic community (or a public sphere of critical spirit) where totalitarianism, authoritarianism, and dogma (or any grand ideology for that matter) are constantly abolished by imagination, interrogation, and (self)-critique.

2

Critical Islam inside Academia

As already explained in the previous chapter, critical Islam does not act under the normative impetus of Western Enlightenment values but merely tries to explain what the normative contents of Islam have been, internalized under specific historical circumstances. This engagement with the text and practice of Islam doubtlessly has political stakes. It comes as a self-reflective interrogation whose addressee is the present moment that has to be liberated from the tyranny of "universal" and "non-historical" theological agendas. In this chapter, I will pay special attention to five different scholarly approaches to the Islamic dogma, all of them trying – with the means of hermeneutic (Muhammed Arkoun, Nasr Abu Zayd), theological (Tariq Ramadan), anthropological (Malek Chebel), and psychoanalytic (Fethi Benslama) analysis – to historicize from within the dogmatic corpora of Islam.

Nasr Abu Zayd was forced to leave Egypt for Holland in the 1990s, right at the peak of the Salman Rushdie controversy and the *hijab affair* in Europe. His scholarship – on the humanistic reception of the Qur'an – attracted the attention of the Western media and his name was frequently cited as an example of "liberal Islam" by journalists, intellectuals, and politicians, defences and critiques of Islam.[1] Forced by a sharia court to divorce his Muslim wife in 1995 (because an apostate cannot be married to a Muslim woman), Nasr Abu Zayd found refuge at the University of Leiden, the Netherlands. He was one of the most important figures in the field of Quranic hermeneutics and a follower of Gadamer and Ricoeur.

Muhammed Arkoun was a Western-educated Muslim intellectual, a professor at the Sorbonne, whose scholarly commitments had always been connected to rethinking the antagonistic relationship

---

Parts of this chapter have been published previously in the *Journal of Religion and Spirituality in Society* (2012, 2015) and in the *Journal of Religion and Society* (2012).

between Islam and the West through a perspective far from the naïve stereotypes of orientalism and far from the heteronomous understanding of Islam that dogmatic theology entertains. Understanding that a possible bridge between cultures, religions, and civilizations is more than a merely reflective exercise, Muhammed Arkoun was an active member of the UNESCO jury of the Prize for Tolerance and Non-violence and an expert collaborator in debates on the *hijab affair* in France in the period 1989–2004, trying to balance the extreme positions of pro and contra activists.[2] Both Nasr Abu Zayd and Muhammed Arkoun passed away in the autumn of 2010 and, in a sense, the comprehensive scholarship on their intellectual heritage and the assessment of their work is still in a nascent state.

Tariq Ramadan, Malik Chebel, and Fethi Benslama are quite different types of scholars from each other and from Arkoun and Abu Zayd; each, nonetheless, I argue, belongs to the Western-Islamic public sphere. Inspired (respectively) by theology, literature and anthropology, and psychoanalysis, the three of them, in different ways, aim to open a public discussion (which should have resonance beyond academia) on the main stakes of historical, dogmatic, and contemporary Islam. Their intellectual work, and their personal biographies, reveal in practice that a new type of community – namely one organized around contested and multiple interpretative strategies of critique and self-critique – is possible. Out of the disparate discursive strategies of negotiating complicated historical legacies is born a new modality of existence and thinking, which is neither purely Western nor purely Islamic, but hyphenated and evasive of all final categorizations: the Western-Islamic public sphere. Moreover, these new public, academically affiliated Western-Muslim intellectuals will reasonably be among the most authoritative scholarly voices of the Western-Islamic public sphere.

Quranic Hermeneutics: The Work of Muhammed Arkoun and Nasr Abu Zayd

The initial purpose of hermeneutics was to explain the word of God. This purpose was eventually expanded into an attempt to explain the process of explaining the word of man. In the nineteenth century we learned, first from Hegel and then more effectively from

Nietzsche, that God is dead. In the twentieth century, Kojève and his students, like Foucault, have informed us that man is dead, thereby as it were opening the gates into an abyss of postanthropological deconstruction. As the scope of hermeneutics has expanded, then the two original meanings, God and man, have vanished taking with them the cosmos or world, leaving us with nothing but our own garrulity which we choose to call the philosophy of language, linguistic philosophy or one of their synonyms. If nothing is real, the real is nothing. There is no difference between the written lines of a text and the blank spaces between them.[3]

Islamic hermeneutics, while a relatively new discipline born in the lecture halls of Western academia,[4] is engaged with a peculiar defense of the sacred text. Neither God nor man is dead within this new tradition of thinking but, rather, they are saved for future life through their de-transcendentalization and historical entanglement. Although (certainly) it is the "divine spirit" of the Qur'an that transcends time and history, its intellectual rescue is possible only if "the letter of the Qur'an" is addressed historically. In the words of Abdel Karim Soroush, "the text does not stand alone, it does not carry its own meaning on its shoulders; it needs to be situated in a context, it is theory-laden, its interpretation is in flux and presuppositions are as actively at work here as elsewhere in the field of understanding."[5]

The moment of revelation for Abu Zayd inevitably secularizes the Qur'an because it places the eternal word of God within human language and history. While the words of Allah, according to the Qur'an are infinite and non-exhaustible, and, therefore, it is impossible that they be confined, the Qur'an itself is only a manifestation – limited in space and time – of the eternal speech of God.[6] Certainly, Abu Zayd follows the ninth-century Mut'azilite school of Sunni Islam, which historically had the most unfortunate destiny in comparison to the other three theological schools in Sunnism (Ash'arite, Hanbalite, and Hanafite).[7] In order to retain the eternal unity of God, the Mut'azilites regard the Qur'an as created: since God is eternal, there cannot be another eternal existence beside Him. The Qur'an, from this perspective, can only be the textual cultural product of seventh-century Arabia and the understanding of its theological characteristics cannot ignore the linguistic peculiarity of Arabic, the social context of the early Islamic community, and the poetic self-referentiality of the Quranic text. It is worth quoting the following passage from Abu Zayd because it captures the essence of his intellectual commitment:

> The Qur'an is then one manifestation of the Word of God to Prophet Muhammad through the mediation of the archangel Gabriel. . . . There should not be any disagreement that the divinity of the Qur'an is confined to its source. The content, however, is strongly correlated with the linguistic structure, which is culturally and historically determined. If the divine content of God's Word has been expressed in human language, it is the domain of language, which is culturally and historically determined. In other words, if the divine content of God's Word has been expressed in human language, it is the domain of language that represents the essential human dimension of all scriptures in general and the Qur'an in particular.[8]

Zayd's reading of the divine text is a political gesture transforming the classical theological concept that insists on the non-createdness of the Qur'an. Man, because of his historicity, is a secular being. However, the atemporal God and the temporal man can communicate because in and through the scripture God has not only revealed Himself but opened Himself to humanity in a common space mediated through history and language. This humanization of the divine is, first, a choice that God has made Himself and, second, as far as the revelation takes place in the linguistic and historical medium, this transformation of the divine, from radical unknowability to the agency of the recitation, is an infinite process. It is important to note that transformation for Abu Zayd does not mean annihilation of Allah but, rather, the emphasis is on the altered relationship between man and God. Paradoxically, the secularization of the Qur'an preserves its theological content because, in the endless conundrums of human language, the pursuit of God is a guaranteed constant renewal. Whatever the theological objections to this approach might be, it is only through the secularization of the Qur'an that its sacredness remains alive and unfinished.

Placing the Qur'an in time and space is also semantically linked to the secular. The word "secular" actually derives from the Latin *saeculum*, which could be translated in English as a historical period, epoch, era, or, more precisely, as the "spirit of time" at the heart of the historical.[9] The secular, therefore, does not only involve the gradual retreat of God from the public domain, but it primarily connotes the advent of a common space in which finite human beings negotiate and deliberate the actions of their finite lives. The secular is the historical and its rejection does not only mean the rejection of history and therefore of the ability of human beings to generate change in their social conditions, but also the rejection of religion insofar as the latter is embodied in series of complicated, historically contingent practices and rituals. From the standpoint of Nasr Abu Zayd's thinking, God enters in communication with man through Muhammed who, after all, is a finite human being; Allah has manifested Himself in human language and, finally, He perpetually involves the believer in the encounter with H/his enigmatic existence in the practice of the Quranic recitation (or prayer) repeated on a daily basis. These are acts that imbricate the divine in the historical flow of time and in the historical polyphony of the social contexts in the house of Islam. In this line of thinking, religious and secular are not antinomies; in fact, dogmatic Islamic theology should be denied the right to define what is *secular* because it is incapable of articulating the ostentatious fact that meaning – individual as well as social – is always historical and discursive; it is always the agreement of a group of people on the terms of their worldly (co)existence.

A quick example of the immediate public stake in historical Quranic hermeneutics is evident in the commentary (which inflicts practice) surrounding one of the most widely disputed verses in the Qur'an: 4:34, on the treatment of women in Islam. The text of the verse in Arabic is stable while its possible translations and interpretations in the course of history have been numerous. Reza Aslan provides two different variants of the verse taken from two of the most authoritative translators of the Qur'an in English. Ahmed Ali, of the Princeton University, interprets the original in the following manner:

> Men are the support of women as God gives some more means than others, and because they spend of their wealth (to provide for them). . . . As for women you feel are averse, talk to them suasively; then leave them alone in bed (without molesting them) and go to bed with them (when they are willing).[10]

The other translation belongs to Majid Fakhry whose publisher is New York University: "Men are in charge of women, because Allah has made some of them excel the others, and because they

spend some of their wealth. . . . And for those women that you feel
might rebel, admonish them and abandon them in their beds and
beat them."[11]

With regard to the hermeneutic reading, the point that both
translations are accurate in terms of grammar and syntax signifies
a proliferation of meanings that must be explored in relation to the
socio-historical context in which the revelation has been received.
Islamic scholarship, since its very beginning in the seventh century, has been male-dominated and patriarchal. The celebrated
eleventh-century Iranian commentator of the Qur'an, Fakhr ad-
Din ar-Razi, for example, interpreted another ambiguous verse,
30:21, as "proof that women were created like animals and plants
and other useful things and not for worship and carrying the
Divine commands . . . because the woman is weak, and in one
sense like a child."[12] The practices that result from similar readings
of the Qur'an, especially violence and death penalties for adulter-
ate partners, are therefore not inherently linked to the Divine text,
which itself is multiple and polyphonic. These readings could only
be secular as long as they are intrinsically linked with the spirit of
the historical time and they should be placed inside its power
dynamics. On the topic of women and the Islamic veil,
Abdelwahab Meddeb, for example, is firm that "the only solution
for women and men who [wish to follow] the Islamic faith while
adapting to the modern [principle] of gender equality is to
acknowledge that all Quranic edicts regarding [women's inferior-
ity] are obsolete and that they are rooted in [historical]
circumstances rather than in [immutable] principles."[13] In a recent
interview for the online edition of the French *Nouvel Observateur*,
Meddeb maintains resolutely:

> The reformers of the late nineteenth century, such as the Egyptian
> Qasim Amin, read the Quranic verses evoked by the clergy for the
> imposition of the veil on women in a quite different way: they [the
> reformers] remind that in these verses it is nowhere said that it is
> necessary the hair and arms to be covered. As for the burqa, it is
> simply absent from the Qur'an. Therefore, everything is a matter
> of interpretation which varies from maximal coercion to maximal
> liberalism, between the refuse of the veil to its fundamentalist adop-
> tion, burqa and niqab. The overwhelming majority of the Islamic
> clergy reads these verses in a sense that imposes the voile on
> women.[14]

At the same time, the Quranic hermeneutics should not be considered an unreflective dismissal of, and condescending political excuse for, all the sexual bias and violence hidden in the divine text. This is not an approach that adopts relativity under the pretext that every historical moment in the existence of Islam has its own peculiar rationale. Even though this observation might be true, the hermeneutic project – at least, the way I read it – is predicated on the idea of self-critique, which can neither fully escape its affectual engagement with the reading of the divine (after all, the Islamic God would not favour the beating of women to death in the twenty-first century) nor fully become the victim of a fossilized set of values equating critique with secularism or Enlightenment rationalism.

Muhammad Arkoun, as the other extremely important figure in the field of hermeneutic Islamic scholarship, offers a different venue for engagement with the Islamic sources. As a French-Arab intellectual, he is involved in the critical re-thinking of the whole of Mediterranean history from the standpoint of Islam's inclusion. At the heart of Arkoun's project lies first the understanding of religion as inherently pluralistic and yet containing a unifying potential for all Muslims, and then something that he calls a "deconstruction of Islamic reason." By "Islamic reason" Arkoun means dogmatic closed reading of the scriptures, obsessed with the utopia of the Pious Ancestor (the first years of the Arabic Caliphate), which deprives the sacred of openness to the future. Similarly to Abu Zayd, Arkoun considers the Islamic tradition paradoxically marked by two opposite processes: linguistic continuity in the transmission of sacred texts and increasing discontinuity in the cultural, social, political, and intellectual fields that comprise the corpus of faith.[15] While the foundational event of Islam is something that Arkoun terms "the Quranic fact" – the moment that places the Islamic revelation in history – the religious tradition itself is fragmentary and dispersed. Islam, therefore, in its multiplicity and fragmentariness, acquires coherence only if it is thought of as an "Islamic fact," which goes beyond the Qur'an itself and includes all the possible social, historical, and discursive practices of Islamic societies. The Islamic fact, for Arkoun, constitutes a discursive field of cultural interaction inside the Greco-Semitic sphere, which is another way of naming the common Mediterranean imaginary where the Latin, Arabic, Berber, and French intellectual heritage find expression.[16]

In the field of religious anthropology, for example, it is particularly important for Arkoun to note that the whole ethico-political definition of man in the Qur'an shares identical definitions with the biblical and evangelical corpora. It is not only the figure of Abraham who binds the three monotheistic religions in a common course within prophetic history but also the alliance of man with the Living and Speaking God. In Islam, man's secret communion with God during prayer raises the human being to the dignity of personhood, while in Christianity (and Judaism) man is ontologically connected with God by image and resemblance. This difference, however important, for Arkoun does not obliterate the fact that God and man enter in communication in both Christianity and Islam. At odds with His classical theological understanding, Allah, for Muhammad Arkoun, is not the radical alterity, the distant and unknowable Absolute, but a loving and speaking God who reveals Himself in temporal history through His prophets and in speech. In that regard, the so-called "mantic" discourse of the revelation – the performative mystic speech of God present in earlier revealed religions – reaches with Islam completely new heights. In the recitation, God and man not only blend in a mystic bond, but the verses contain intrinsic emancipatory potential and are self-referentiality loaded with the auto-poesis of the divine.[17]

On the religious plane, Islam as the last monotheistic religion (the last of the People of the Book) ends the prophetic chain through the introduction of Muhammad as the Seal of the Prophets, which is an important contribution to the development of the history of salvation in monotheism. At the same time, the historical uniqueness of Islam as a social practice and faith is truly revealed only when thought as part of a larger history. The Mediterranean imaginary, which acquires density through the complicated memories in the region from the time of the Muslim, Byzantine, and Western Christian empires, is the prism that Arkoun adopts. The Mediterranean is unique, therefore, because it is a space constituted around shared symbolic capital: the revelation has dominated for centuries the political realm while the jihad/crusades – the armed action. In the modern period, after the dissolution of the Ottoman Empire, notes Arkoun, the hegemonic West penetrates deeply into the house of Islam through the processes of colonization and decolonization, and, up until the present day, the histories and practices of Islam and the West are still intertwined in a more-than-simple historical bond. While the region integrates the sacred histories of monotheism, it is also a common yet vibrant and fractured space of antagonisms and pen-

etrations. The battle of Lepanto (1571) for Arkoun is one historical example of how the secular and sacred histories of
Mediterranean societies are intertwined in a shared symbolic continuum, which, even today, determines the stereotypical division
between the Islamic East and the Christian West, as well as some
of the rhetoric in the Israeli-Palestinian conflict.[18] Despite all the
divisions, however, Arkoun insists academics and public intellectuals should join their efforts in thinking this space as one in which
Islam belongs – in history and today – irreversibly. Only if multiple and dispersed practices of Islam, represented through the
notions Quranic fact and Islamic fact in the sacred and mundane
realm, become recognized as internal parts of a shared Western-
Islamic history, the "Muslim minorities living in European and
American societies (will) be included in the general exploration of
attitudes and approaches to civil societies."[19] This same vision of
one Mediterranean world in which Islam plays a vital role is somewhat continued by Abdelwahab Meddeb in an interview for the
German newspaper *Die Ziet* in relation to Pope Benedict XVI's
lecture in Germany (September 12, 2006) at the University of
Regensburg.[20] Here, Meddeb, while evoking the role of Turkey in
Europe, elegantly shifts the focus to the Arab world:

> Turkey. Its status as part of Europe is a matter of survival for us.
> Admitting the Turks into the EU would provide essential confirma-
> tion of the solidity of our principles, which are not just
> Judeo-Christian, but which contain a mighty historical promise of
> convergence. . . . But I also think Morocco is on the right path, even
> if it has seen no republican awakening like Turkey. As a result of the
> French influence, the whole of the northern Mediterranean region is
> suited to becoming a laboratory of European thought. Only here can
> we win the worldwide cultural battle against the Islamists.[21]

It is obvious, therefore, that the Quranic hermeneutics escapes
"the abyss of postanthropological deconstruction" through politi-
cizing its message, or, more accurately, through historicizing it. The
Qur'an is a divine text, certainly, from the standpoint of the believer
(in the way other sacred texts are considered divine for other
communities), but what institutes this text as divine, i.e. what makes
it constitutive for the social imaginary of Muslims, is a historical
argument engaging a multifarious historical process. While it is true
that the sacred text is a pure embodiment of the deepest poesis of

the social and it is communicative of the politics of the divine, as Bataille or Walter Benjamin would argue, it is still more important to understand how this text has been authorized historically as sacred. Actually, the fact that it is considered sacred does not necessarily mean that it is truly revealed by God and it does not mean that it should not be secularized through the infinite (self-)critique of the scholarly mind. At the same time, the Quranic hermeneutics – through its methodology and assumptions – is by all means a founding gesture of the Western-Islamic public sphere, insofar as it opens a space of thinking of these two terms – Islam and the West – first, in their historical complexities and then, in their infinite openness to future interventions.

The Scholarly Projects of Tariq Ramadan, Malek Chebel, and Fethi Benslama

The public debate on religion, initiated by Western Muslim intellectuals, occurring on the boundaries of various disciplines and exploiting various vocabularies, is crucial for any attempt at understanding and deconstructing the East-West division. This debate has not only theoretical but also pragmatic dimensions. Critical Islam encounters the secularist state (especially in the French case) with intellectual arguments that did not remain unnoticed given the intensity of the public exchange and the subsequent legislative measures. Let us see how the three different modes of thinking, shown in Ramadan, Chebel, and Benslama, get involved in the process of political praxis.

Tariq Ramadan suggests that a public sphere centered on the generation of public opinion, even when the interlocutors do not constitute a *demos* in the narrow political sense of the word, is legitimate if it has a universal normative basis, one that only religion and no other normative power may yield. Ramadan overtly declares that Western public spheres lose their cohesive force and political thrust and practically dismantle into fragmented, disparate, and alienated discourses under increasing transnational pressures because they have never questioned their normative secular underpinnings. Ramadan's project is declared to be anti-secularist and anti-secular but when one carefully reads his program agenda, the worldly substance of his theology becomes more palpable.

Malek Chebel, psychoanalyst and anthropologist of Islam, is committed to developing, in a series of fundamental theoretical works, a complicated historical-literary-psychoanalytic commentary on the traditions of love, sexuality, and gender divisions in Islam that culminates in a complex "pedagogy of love" in the words of Ruth Mas, a major researcher of Chebel's thought.[22] Chebel's work, which aims to de-essentialize Islam by re-thinking the historical relation between Islam and the West, has gained popularity in France at a moment when the French public sphere has become bitterly vulnerable in regards to secularity. At the risk of a hasty generalization, I would like to suggest that Chebel is attacking the non-negotiable supremacy of European civilization's integration of Christianity and secularism by placing Islam inside the European narrative. While Ramadan's critique stresses that the Islamic cosmopolis and the universalism of the Muslim *ummah* are compatible with modernity, Chebel perceives the integration of Islam and the West through the "positing of sex at the crucible of the Islamic religion."[23]

Finally, Fethi Benslama, a French-Arab psychoanalyst, similarly focuses on the complicated Islam-West relationship in his recent book *Psychoanalysis and the Challenge of Islam*. Unlike Chebel, however, Benslama is interested in the origin of Islam as represented in the central theological corpuses of Islam and Christianity. Paradigmatic for both Islam and Christianity is the parable of the triad of Abraham, Sarah, and Hagar and the consequent birth of Abraham's two sons, Ishmael and Isaac. While Isaac was conceived by divine intervention – by the will of God as a response to Sarah's desperation at her sterility and childlessness – Ishmael occurs naturally as a result of copulation between Abraham and Hagar. According to *Genesis*, Abraham is the symbolic father of the Judeo-Christian tradition because Sarah's child is an exception, something external to the natural law. By contrast, Abraham is the real father of Ishmael and of Islam, which means that Allah, neither giving birth nor being born, functions in a completely different way than the God of Judaism and Christianity. The God of Islam is not an originary father, a fact that places Him in a unique, trans-parental position according to Benslama. This radical alterity in Islam is extremely important for all debates on Islam and the public sphere because it reflects a concept of absolute sovereignty that is foreign to the historical, political, and religious trajectory of Western secularization.[24]

Tariq Ramadan

Tariq Ramadan, a significant Egyptian-Swiss Islamic philosopher, is a major intellectual figure who has appeared on the international scene due to his active presence on the internet, on television, and on tape recordings. Ramadan's personal website, for example, is a kind of information portal that assembles and transmits in several languages information, videos, lectures, debates, and controversies that concern global Islam. The site is also a public forum, where issues from theology to social practices, from Islam as spiritual horizon to Islam as sexual practice and lifestyle, are contested and discussed.[25]

Ramadan's articles in the Western press, originally written in relation to the *hijab affair* in France, have become central to public debates in Western societies. Questioning the legitimacy of secularism and republicanism, Ramadan is also concerned with the education of European and Western Muslims in the ethics of citizenship based upon Muslim principle.[26] Ramadan is the perfect example of the diasporic intellectual because his ideas are not limited to spatial or territorial sovereignty. By overcoming "soil" and "place," the program that Ramadan advocates consolidates around trans-local principles of solidarity and offers a collective religious idiom for the framing of a post-national Muslim identity.

Clearly, Ramadan's political agenda is projected as a new, critical re-thinking of a thousand-year-old perspective on the construction of the critical subject and citizen who acts on the transnational level. Many Muslims living in the West have experienced an authentic intellectual revolution nourished by their historic responsibilities and resuscitated by the opportunities and challenges they have confronted: the citizens of democratic states enjoy higher levels of education and have become more critical in their dedication to faith, ethics, and tradition; new generations of men and women populate the political landscape of Western countries.[27]

Though Ramadan's reflections appear analytical, they are also, like most political discourses, a program, a call to mobilize critical Muslim voices to adopt democratic methods of action, starting at the local level. This appeal aims to lighten the burden of traditional Islamic authority by taking advantage of decentralized and competing modalities of Islamic traditions and institutions. All such attempts, however, face the difficult task of achieving a balance between reconstructing and democratizing tradition, on the one hand, and acknowledging the bitter vulnerability of Europe and the West on the topic of secularity, on the other.

A delicate moment in Tariq Ramadan's argument is the need to reconcile the appeal for democratic participation with the reconstruction of sharia in a way that will allow the application of *fiqh* (Islamic law) in a form suitable to practicing believers in Western societies.[28] According to the approach of critical Islam, the stake is not limited to establishing order in the lives of Western Muslims; it also presupposes the implementation of practical platforms for the inclusion of Muslims as citizens on the basis of a "common good" shared with non-Muslim citizens. In other words, Muslim law should not define the dimensions of good and bad only for Muslims; the law should be interpreted in a way that encompasses humanity in general. Ramadan argues that such an approach would prevent the ghettoizing of Muslim communities. Thus, the concept of sharia as the supreme law connecting all Muslims is not negated; rather, it is interpreted in ways that emphasize connectedness through the common good over the casuistic essence of the key normative Islamic platform.

The universality of the Muslim *ummah* together with an acute sensitivity towards a need for reform similar to the reform impulses that mobilized the Islamic world during the nineteenth century inspired Tariq Ramadan's engagement with the question of the compatibility of Islam and modernity. A key idea for Ramadan, however, is that the spirit of Islam has penetrated Europe, which implies not only the successful integration of Islam into the secular universe of the West but also the West's acceptance of an Islamic spirit that has already deeply penetrated European societies. At the same time, being a European Muslim, for Ramadan, means an indispensable dedication to the Islamic tradition.

Malek Chebel

A completely different articulation of Islam, though still unorthodox and approached from a new angle on the Islam-modernity relationship, is that of Malek Chebel: "Love itself. The capacity to love, that is one of the aims of my analysis. In other words, the capacity to enter into relation."[29] The audience that Malek Chebel's work (written in

French) addresses is generally the Franco-Maghrebi population of the French republic. Having deviated from the norms of conservative Islam, the Franco-Maghrebis are, in the words of Tariq Ramadan, "European Muslims without Islam,"[30] who ethically and culturally do not belong to the Arabic and Islamic hinterlands. At the same time, it is important to mention that the social and cultural practices of the French-Maghrebi population, no matter how deviant and emergent they may seem as a result of their immigrant compromises, maintain a high profile in the dominant French culture. Apart from the historically strong public influence of the French orientalist school, the figure of the Islamic intellectual has occupied a special place in the French reading and writing elite since 1989, an important year in the international coverage of Islam due to two significant media-intensive events, the fatwa issued against Salman Rushdie by Ayatollah Khomeini and the *hijab affair* in France. After 1989, the Islamic intellectual crystallized into four distinct types in the French public sphere: The vanguard intellectual who acquires popularity through artistic and political activity is an important category, populated by public figures converted to Islam and intellectuals from the Muslim world: Youssouf Leclerc, Jean-Loup Abdelhalim Herbert, Vincent Monteil, Eva de Vitray-Meyerovitch, Mohamed Dib, Mohamed Harbi, Nasser Pakdaman, Haytham Manna, Shunsuddin Guzel, Lotfallah Soliman, and Abbas Baydoun are some of the members of this category. Another category, the one of most interest to my analysis, is the so-called intellectual reformer; Tariq Ramadan, who did not emerge from the French intellectual elite, is an example of this because of his frequent and significant activism and presence in French media. However, although they follow different professional pathways, intellectuals such as Fatima Mernissi, Abdelmajid Charfi, Nasr Abou-Zayd, Youssef Seddik, Abdul Karim Soroush, Abdou Filali-Ansary, Abdelwahab Meddeb, Malek Chebel, and Farid Esack are thinkers who are prepared to reform Islam from 'the inside,' and are therefore of this category as well. The Maghrebi thinkers are so well represented that Algeria, Tunis, and Morocco are considered "the Islamic soil where the voice which calls for a new approach to the religious phenomenon is the most distinct."[31] The works of Chebel, Benslama, Muhammad Arkoun, Abdou Filali-Ansary, Fatima Mernissi, and Rachid Benzine are exemplary in their insistence that the Maghreb re-appear as a critical and intellectual alternative to orthodox Islam. The other two categories of Muslim intellectual, important as they are, could be defined as intellectual-representatives of French Islam (as are Sheikh Abbas, Abdullah Ben Mansour, and Farid Abdelkarim, the leaders of France's mosque federations) and Muslim intellectuals who are socio-political leaders in France (as are Herlem Desir, the president of the NGO *SOS Racism*, and Fadela Amara, a feminist writer, a minister in the cabinet of Nicolas Sarkozy, and a leader of the civil movement *Ni putes ni Soumises* [Fr. Neither Whores nor Oppressed]).[32]

Chebel's general point is that Islam is plural in form, practice, and content. For Chebel, Islam is the main constituent of a complex and originally multiple Arabo-Islamic, Mediterranean Oriental civilization comprised of a mosaic of populations such as Arabs, Berber tribes, Latinized and Christianized segments, and Jewish minorities. Islam is an extremely important prism for understanding the essence of this civilization, but Chebel also believes it should be thought through the prism of this inherent plurality that diversifies and multiplies its face from the inside. What is more, Chebel considers the discourse of love primordial in discussing Islamic alterity and the radical Other. In his seminal book *The Arab-Islamic Imaginary*, with a tentative and nuanced dedication, Malek Chebel elaborates on the complex amalgam of concepts and practices that constitute Islamic love. First of all, love in Islam is a triad that unites, sometimes awkwardly, affection (*houbb*), passion (*'ichq*), and desire (*chawq*).[33] Deviating from the purely Quranic reading that defines divine love as *houbb*, Chebel's ambition is to intertwine the love of Allah (*mahibba*) with the completely heterogeneous and immanent dimension of Islam's visions of human love and sexual practice. This theoretical demarche is further developed in Chebel's 1995 *Encyclopedia of Love in Islam* and in his 2001 book *A Hundred Names of Love*, which is not only dedicated to the Islamic Eros but is also a bold wink from the author to the ninety-nine names of God in the Qur'an. Especially severe is Chebel's critique of Islamic jurisprudence's restrictions on sexual practices, insisting that literalist interpretations create an oppressed world of love, eroticism, and sexual indulgence that nourishes an Eros at the margins, a universe of "sexual perversities and marginalities"[34] that is deviant but nonetheless fundamental to the plurality of Maghrebi Islam. This particular perspective leads Chebel to reflect on the demystification of heterosexual love as an ideal and the thesis that the persecution of homosexuality in Islam and the sacralization of female virginity are ignorant of the multiple practices of love in Islam's royal societies and literary tradition dating as far back as the poetry of Al-Jahiz (775–869). In fact, the Qur'an, the hadith tradition, the life and example of the Prophet himself, and the rich poetic and literary heritage of Islam provide testimony that "there is nothing vile in taking interest in bodily things when the spirit and the soul are bursting with religious conviction and nourished with sincere faith."[35] Chebel's whole 'theology' is inspired by Mut'azilite readings, more particularly by their belief in the createdness of the Qur'an and its openness to hermeneutic interpretation.

Certainly, Chebel's work has had strong political reverberations in France. Unlike Tariq Ramadan, Malek Chebel strongly supports the French government in its attempt to ban all public religious expression and is one of the proponents of the thesis that the *hijab* is nefarious to female dignity. Usually reproached as a traitor by interlocutors such as Ramadan and accused of being a defender of the radical, militant version of French secularism, Malek Chebel engages with Islam in a way more complicated and worthwhile than press labels and narrow political clichés. Chebel is clearly of the view that Islam has no other option but to diversify and subject to historical-critical analysis its basic tenets and prescriptions. However, it would be extremely simplistic and unfair to ignore Chebel's profound criticism of the Western project of modernity, which crystallizes in between the lines of his preoccupation with Islam. Chebel does not privilege secularist over religious reasoning (as Ruth Mas does, for example) but rather explores their entanglement in the complicated project of modernity from a post-structuralist perspective.

A major fact for Chebel is that the Enlightenment, modernity, and secularism have all been catalyzed by religion. No matter how powerfully Islam is subject to assimilation and secularization in the Western milieu, it cannot be stripped of its social, cultural, and philosophical role: partial, plural, heterogeneous, and multiple, Islam is nonetheless a call to universality, a reservoir of humanity's hope amidst its most deeply felt injustices. Even though the practices and truths of Islam are plural for Malek Chebel, the Islamic religion is neither functionally superfluous nor incapable of being a remedy to the acutely felt malaise of modernity. Multifarious Islam, Islam of the marginal, of the poets and of the outcasts, in the final analysis means the multifarious operation of reason and memory and a delicate escape from reason's instrumental and strategic action.

All of the academic representatives of critical Islam share a moment of disenchantment with both the project of modernity and the dogmas of religion. This state of disenchantment initiates a critique that is less a rejection of religion than its modification and alteration. One of the main utopias of the modern world is one where societies and individuals may choose between Athens and Jerusalem, between the rationality of ancient Greece that has informed the historically convoluted path of secularization in the West and faith in the One as encoded in Christianity. Obviously, the question that the academic branch of critical Islam asks, although indirectly, is where is Mecca in this configuration?

Fethi Benslama

The Islamic cosmopolis of Tariq Ramadan is one possible answer (even though the least convincing from the standpoint of the Western-Islamic public sphere), while Malek Chebel's "geography of love in Islam" is a different type of engagement. Fethi Benslama is the only one of the three thinkers who dares to ask this question overtly in his writing; *Psychoanalysis and the Challenge of Islam* takes as a theoretical prism the experimental tradition of the psychoanalytic construction. The aim is to open and explore in a non-banal way the vast literary, ethical, theological, and ontological archive of Islam. Central for Fethi Benslama is the problem of origin, where Islam is placed in a historical, theological, and philosophical affinity with the Judeo-Christian monotheistic tradition. However, a significant difference between Islam and Judeo-Christianity is the fact that the God of Islam is not a father. This means for Benslama that Allah, excluded from the logic of paternity, functions as an absolute sovereign, as an absolute *différance* with no human reference whatsoever. Abraham is the "real" father of Islam since his first-born son, Ishmael, stays at the origin of the Arab genealogy.[36] An especially provocative moment is Benslama's observation that Ishmael becomes an Arab when Muhammad names him as such: only in speech does Ishmael become the head of the genealogy of Islam, meaning that fiction marks the very beginning of the original narrative.

The God of Islam is not the result of sexual relations, insists Benslama, nor does He appear in the Qur'an through symbolic filiation. Allah is incommensurable with any reference from this world; he withdraws, and, through his withdrawal, the place of the father is opened. Therefore, Benslama's point is that God in Islam is actually the original withdrawal of the father.[37] It is precisely this peculiarity in the very mechanism of the functioning of the divine, this "limit of writing the origin"[38] (as God is not the father but, paradoxically, at the very origin of Islam is the naturally conceived son of Abraham and Hagar) that constitutes the radical alterity of Islam. Allah is the complete, irreducible Other. This absolute sovereignty of God is further manifested in one of the Arabic expressions for God, *huwa huwa*, which literally means "he is another self in himself": He is He.[39]

How does the nature of "He" become knowable if God Himself does not participate in the Man–Father relation? If the father is not God Himself, then, an important characteristic of Islam is the impossibility for man to identify with God's essence; the divine is always external to the human. However, the God-man relationship is even more complicated than this preliminary reading suggests because the Arabic word for "essence" and "identity," *huwiya*, is derived from the third-person singular *huwa*, which is, as mentioned, one of the names for God. Identity and essence are therefore brought by recourse to the divine, which seems to be radically divorced from any human reference. For Fethi Benslama, this radical alterity of Islam, this double bind that exists in Islam in the essence of the relationship between man and his God, puts the individual believer in the absolutely new situation of identifying with something impossible. The Islamic God cannot be achieved: he is a potentiality that the individual and historical believer strives to achieve incessantly in his immanence and imperfection, but the final achievement of the divine is always suspended; it is, in the end, impossible.

In a 1998 text called *The Veil of Islam* (*La voile d'islam*), Fethi Benslama initiates a psychoanalytic commentary on the condition of women according to Islam. His engagement was provoked by the ardent debates in France over the ban of religious symbols, a topic that has commanded public attention and passion in Europe since 1989. Benslama's analysis begins with a remark made in 1994 by the Minister of Education, Mr. Francois Bayrou, who, while expressing deep respect for Islam as a religion and cultural system, declared in *Libération* that "the face of France" was in danger due to the widespread public visibility of the *hijab*. The Islamic veil (and the face behind it) is thus a stand-in here for the "face of France" and functions in these debates as a synonym for integralism (fundamentalism) versus integration. A significant misunderstanding in the French debate concerns the nature of the Islamic veil as a religious symbol. From a strictly theological perspective, the veil is not a sign but an anti-sign, as it is not the veil but the female body that indicates too much. "Veiling is thus the operation of the negation of the body of a woman. Through this operation, woman is elevated into a forbidden or sacred thing, that is to say, into an ideality which at the same time preserves a sensible existence."[40] Furthermore, Benslama recalls the paradigmatic story of Muhammad and Khadija: Khadija is the first Muslim because she is the first one who believed in the Prophet and his message. Through Khadija, Muhammad entered into certitude about his God because she was the first one to recognize the speech of Archangel Gabriel as the truth of the Other. She is veiled while Muhammad shares his possession with her, but the moment of unveiling makes the angel flee, a testimony of his truth. In the final account, Khadija re-veils herself as a gesture of acceptance and obeisance before this same truth. In fact, initiating a close reading of theology means acknowledging that being woman means being complicit with the truth of the Other, which she reaffirms through the veiling that suspends her and the Other vis-à-vis one another in the mystery of the Quranic revelation. This semiology of the veil is further complicated when Ayesha, Muhammad's favorite wife, separates from the tribe in order to look for a necklace in the desert, followed by Safwan, with whom Ayesha had an affair before becoming Muhammad's spouse. This throws the Prophet into a torment of jealousy. After Ayesha's clearing, the veil becomes a whole social order that structures not only the female body but relations between people, the public, and private space.

Why are Benslama's re-interpretations of basic moments in Islamic theology important for and, in a sense foundational to, the project of a Western-Islamic public sphere? It is obvious that two regimes of truth are competing for the same space. On the one hand, there is the "truth" of the French state as embodied in its various educative and public institutions that define as their aim the "defense of the face of France" through the reinforcement of the French *laïcité* and the rights of man; on the other, there is the truth of the Muslim girl who wants to preserve her modesty before her God. The clash of these two universalisms is the kernel of the conflict. Moreover, this conflict generates an image of the Other on the other side of the barricade through various prohibitions and institutionalizations that are primordial for the functioning of any community. As Benslama puts it, "There is no other without the prohibition that makes him other to himself and to the other. Prohibition is the institution of the other."[41]

Critical Perspective – Part I

One way to read both religious ideologies, therefore, is through being aware of their absolute heteronomy where all authority is predicated on self-enclosed, self-supported, and unquestionable externality suspended in the ahistorical void: God is transcendent; His power is absolute, eternal, and not susceptible to human interventions. This particular understanding of religion is not only fundamentalist – and the Western-Islamic public sphere is a project meant to take a position against it – but also it shares the same conceptual terrain with the glorious rationalist notion of pure autonomy in its Kantian version. Pure autonomy, similarly to pure heteronomy, signifies the tautological, self-referential identity of the theological mind (regardless of whether the latter is defined in religious or secularist terms). Using different scholarly regimes, the Muslim intellectuals whose work was discussed in this chapter suggest that such an allegedly 'autonomous' subject cannot be historically, politically, or ontologically represented because it is hermetic and unchanging. It cannot be in history – it is always outside all historical contingencies and alterations – because it lacks any self-changing powers and, at its best, it could be contemplated, worshipped, or renounced by someone else who considers their being derived from it.[42] Critical Islam offers a different itinerary of religion and freedom. Autonomy and heteronomy, along with the notion of intellectual critique, frame to a large extent the language that I use to define the Western-Islamic public sphere. The *heteronomous* God has to be brought back – secularized, in a sense – at the centre of human possibility.[43] And, human *autonomy*, on the other hand, has to be conceived as a project of self-critique and self-alteration; a true project of autonomy is perpetually open to its own failures and transformations, which makes it experimental and autopoetic in nature.[44] It is not evident what kind of social imaginary and under what socio-historical circumstances such a project of autonomy would come into being. History has witnessed the multiple failures of all kinds of theological, secularist, or humanist regimes of power. The Western-Islamic public sphere is one possible alternative for the observation and analysis of present-day religious controversies. It is an intellectual tool for understanding controversies related to the public presence and the visibility of Islam in the West. The Western-Islamic public sphere is an intellectual universe committed to autonomy through the praxis of the radical interrogation of all inalienable and unchangeable truths.

3

North-American Post-Colonial Studies and European Polemics against Islam

The intellectual projects of Nasr Abu Zayd, Muhammad Arkoun, Tariq Ramadan, Malik Chebel, and Fethi Benslama, different as they may be, share a commitment to de-stabilizing from within the fossilized and atemporal dogmata of classical and/or fundamentalist Islamic theology. While their critique employs different strategies – historical analysis, Quranic exegesis, and anthropological, literary, and psychoanalytic analysis – to communicate that Islam is complicated, plurivocal, and existent inside the secularized historical flow of events, their engagement has been regarded, in academia and beyond, with extreme suspicion. Confusion exists as to the precise addressee of critical Islam – indigenous Islamic audiences, the Western interlocutor, or both – and how the message has been received inside the different and disparate publics it inevitably reaches. The central polemics are about the politics of critical Islam and its possible involvement with two oppositional camps of thought and action.

On the one hand, critical Islam has been accused of being in alliance with secularist liberal imperial hegemonies embodied, according to the arguments of Saba Mahmood and Talal Asad, by the United States or the liberal West in general. For Mahmood, it is obvious that Quranic hermeneutics, or critical Islam in my terms, is a new type of hegemony, which springs from within Islam and, masked as liberating intellectualism, not only generates self-colonizing narratives for the fundamentalist, irrational, ahistorical Muslim, but also serves the political interests of the Western empire in a post-9/11 world. In that regard, it is not coincidental that critical Islam is a Western academic discourse because it emerges as a logical continuation of classical orientalist power constellations: the theocratic and religious "them" versus the democratic, liberal, and secularist "us." Currently generated by a bunch of 'liberal' Muslims, the approach of critical Islam, Mahmoud maintains, does not take into consideration the anthropological, lived experience of Islam today with its indigenous grammars and explanations of Islamist and fundamentalist revival, and it therefore should be exposed as a discourse nourished by the normative (obviously external to "authentic Islam" for Mahmood) impetus of secularism. Following the argument in Mahmood's ethnography *Politics of Piety*, which provides an account of the women's mosque movement in Cairo in the mid-nineties, one is left with the impression that for Mahmood the anonymous and apolitical women in three Cairo mosques, who seem to adopt and enhance the patriarchal logic of fundamentalist Islam, have more to say about the 'proper' reading of the Qur'an than the Western Muslim professors, especially those specializing in Quranic hermeneutics.[1] It seems also that, for Mahmood, the lived experience of Islam in the practices of these women is less prone to political instrumentalizations – despite the fact that they support Islamic fundamentalism – than the educated discourse of the Sorbonne professors. Compelling and rigorous as it might be, the argument of Saba Mahmood seems caught in the ahistorical binaries of orientalism with little or no attention paid to the complexity – biographical, political, and religious – that informs the commitments of the Muslim intellectuals whose work she ardently denounces – one of her targets is Nasr Abu Zayd – in the article "Secularism, Hermeneutics and Empire: the Politics of Islamic Reformation."[2] My contention, contrary to what Mahmood suggests, is that critical Islam is thinkable only if one takes into consideration its critical engagement both with the West and the local Islamic traditions. Critical Muslim intellectuals, from my perspective, attack vehemently those ideologies of secularism that deny Islam a merited place within Western histories, but they adopt, indeed, the *secular* as a critical theoretical perspective connecting Islam and the West in an open, historical, de-transcendentalized relationship. This gesture, I argued in the previous two chapters, is foundational to the theory and praxis of the Western-Islamic public sphere.

On the other hand, critical Islam is frequently taken for fundamentalism camouflaged in liberal rhetoric. While many efforts have been devoted to prove that these accusations have certain relevance to Tariq Ramadan's theology,[3] there is still an enormous amount of suspicion towards the general ability of Islam and its educated representatives in Europe to break from fundamentalist theology and propose a tolerant framework of engagement. For a number of European intellectuals and critiques of Islam, for example, the public demands of the Islamic religion speak not only to the failure of any attempt at multiculturalism, but also put an unjust moral pressure on Europe, in particular, to redefine its intellectual heritage and history. *The Tyranny of Guilt: An Essay on Western Masochism*, written by Pascal Bruckner, is probably the book that best describes the feeling of resentment and resistance to Islam in Europe. While it is historically true that Europe was involved in fascism, communism, genocide, slavery, racism, and imperialism – the sites of guilt for Bruckner – now it is more important than ever to say that the European civilization also invented, for each, the means of their abolition and denounced them through practices yet unachievable in other, non-Western, parts of the world. From Bruckner's perspective, Western Islam capitalizes on the memory and guilt of Europe in order to demand privileges incompatible with the universal liberal ideals of the West. At the same time, with regard to the postcolonial rhetoric targeting the Western empire, Bruckner protests: "Colonialism has . . . become a portmanteau word that no longer designates a specific historical process but everything that is rejected – the Republican ideal, the French model, secularism, the influence of the multinationals, and who knows what else?"[4]

I chose to discuss Pascal Bruckner's extremely provocative arguments here for a couple of reasons. First, Bruckner belongs to the circle of the *New Philosophers* in France, who, before 1989, had been interested in finding what motivates the support of Western intellectuals for communism, the Soviet Union, China, Cuba, and other similar regimes, in the context of increasing evidence of the oppressive structures of these regimes. Whatever motivated the sympathies of Western intellectuals for oppressive and reactive ideologies in the past – and in Bruckner's terms these sympathies could be explained through a historical analysis of the notions "third worldism," the "noble savage," and "utopia" – it reappears today in the form of Western discourses on multiculturalism that support, rather than denounce, radical Islam. Here and elsewhere, Bruckner severely criticizes both the Islamic public political demands and Western intellectuals – mostly, Ian Buruma, Timothy Garton Ash, and Olivier Roy – for their ungrounded support for Tariq Ramadan and

"Western" Islam, and for their failure to recognize the fundamentalist rhetoric behind false messages of tolerance. Bruckner's arguments, therefore, are important because they provide insight into the dynamics of the European reception of Islam in general and into some internal intricacies related to the legitimacies of the term "critical Islam." His work also focuses on the responsibilities of the intellectual work – Muslim and Western – in general.

Second, Pascal Bruckner's indignation towards the advances of Islam in Europe – and he is particularly supportive of American politics in the domain of Islam – could be read as an imaginary response to Saba Mahmood's fears that Islam in post-9/11 Western political constellations is reduced to the silent, oppressed, and anonymous term, this time around with the help of ersatz Muslim intellectualism. Bruckner, on the contrary, would argue that in this same post-9/11 world "there is also a despotism on the part of the minorities who resist assimilation,"[5] who "think that France is a nation whose past is ignoble and whose ideals are repugnant, who see it as a simply provider of services in which one has all rights and no duties,"[6] which rehabilitates Islam as privileged and all-empowered in Western settings. Actually, Mahmood's polemic against intellectual Islam is anthropological: intellectuals create discursive hegemonies that support political hegemonies with no attention to the multiple practices of real Islam. Bruckner's argument, among other things, is a counter-response to this call for anthropology "from below" because certain fundamentalist Islamic practices are, in fact, for him, detestable, oppressive, and non-liberal (to say the least), and Europe has already paid too much attention to them. In Bruckner's perspective, Western, presumably secular, intellectuals' support for Islamic dogmatism paves the way for fundamentalist religious theology in European politics – a contention that should not only be named but fiercely resisted. "In Europe, either Islam will become one religion among others or it will collide with strong resistance on the part of free people for whom the yoke of fanaticism, two centuries after the French revolution, is intolerable."[7]

The Western-Islamic public sphere offers a site of encounter for the two opposing arguments insofar as it exposes them as insensitive to the historical developments that they both try to protect and defend. While it is true that historically the West embraced and forced imperialistic policies in the Orient in various ways – through technocratic rationalism, educational content, and administrative bureaucracies, through the imposition of Western cultural ego ideals, civilizational mores, and secularist politics – it is also true that the European empires, again in the same historical period, disciplined and terrorized in a similar way their own populations. Only knowledge about the complexity of the historical context, Western and non-Western alike, can actually help us understand precisely how, and to what extent, the empire modified and violated the subjectivities of the colonized people. After all, the representatives of critical Islam, perfectly fluent in French and English, defend Islam today in the face of the former colonizer. Saba Mahmood and Talal Asad – the most passionate critiques of the Western forms of power and defenders of the 'authentic Islam' and representatives of a certain Muslim intellectual elite – are actually both professors in prestigious American universities.

In the context of this book, the most problematic assumption endorsed in the postcolonial circles of the North American academia (of which Mahmood and Asad are emblematic figures) is that the imperial and the secular are equivalent terms. My conviction here is that both the secular and the political (religious, imperial, liberal, etc.) must be explored through the complexity of their historical relationship. This is the reason why the distinction between *secular* and *secularist* made in the first chapter seems particularly important. In the context of the Western-Islamic public sphere, critical Islam is anti-secularist but nonetheless secular. The *secular* – which is etymologically related to the historical – as mobilized in critical Islam, it seems to me, acts against empire because it militates to prove that Islam is internal to Western civilizational formations. On the other hand, the extreme refusal on the part of Bruckner to recognize that the demands of Western Islam today, no matter if they are framed as intellectual, religious, or communal, seems equally reductive and misleading.

The Conundrums of Orientalism: The Reception of Critical Islam in North American Academia

Saba Mahmood's article "Secularism, Hermeneutics and Empire: the Politics of Islamic Reformation" was the center of a symposium organized in 2007 at the Townsend Center for the Humanities at the University of California, Berkeley. Later on, the article's controversial reception continued with the Social Science Research Council's invitation to all the conference participants to publish their contributions as a response to *The Immanent Frame*'s question "Is Critique Secular?" I am particularly inspired here by the exchange between Saba Mahmood and Stathis Gourgouris on the topic of secularism. Focused particularly on Mahmood's misreading and political instrumentalization of the hermeneutic argument, I would like to confess theoretical solidarity with Gourgouris's understanding of the *secular* as an emancipatory project open to historical alterations versus *secularism*, an institutional term that has acted in history under the constraints of ahistorical and asocial agendas of various heteronomous – liberalist, legalist, rationalist, imperialist etc. – argumentations.[8]

It seems that Saba Mahmood, in "Secularism, Hermeneutics and Empire: the Politics of Islamic Reformation," has several important points to make in support of the thesis that American secularist and liberalist politics in the Middle East legitimize themselves through discursive strategies borrowed by secular Quranic hermeneutics. First, Mahmood develops the classical orientalist statement: American liberalism (empire or hegemony in Said's terms) is a formidable mould of institutional and linguistic practices embodied in a complicated imperial state apparatus that is normatively secularist; specifically, it is the secularist assumption that underlies the contemporary American involvement with Islam. It aims to forcefully secularize Islamic subjectivities and is observable through analysis of the Rand Corporation Reports, a conservative American think tank with a key role in shaping the US foreign policy after World War II, and also a fervent advocate of "secular theology" for the Middle East after 9/11.[9] In the article in question, as well as in a later post for SSRC, Mahmood entirely conflates the terms secular and secularist, liberalist, and imperialist without being attentive to the different epistemological terrains that inform them. With regard to the secular, Mahmood is certainly indebted to her tutor, Talal Asad, whose work has engaged for years with the so-called "anthropology of the secular." In this tradition, the secular and the religious are seen as coterminous yet in vertical power dependency. For Asad, the secular, naturally in the course of Western history, became a political characteristic of the modern state, which appeared not to abolish but to control religion through the disciplining apparatus of the civil institutions.[10] These historical transformations related mostly to the rise of the institutional apparatus of the modern bureaucracies altered the secular into a secularist ideology. Therefore, Mahmood insists, echoing Asad, that the *saeculum* in the secular – namely the time component in saeculum – is related to "premodern" meanings that oppressive modern practices obliterate.[11] Time and history, however, are also categories of modernity and no matter how much postmodern scholars deconstruct them or apply to them strategies of relativization – those strategies, actually, analytically ground the whole field of postcolonial studies – they contain the critical emancipatory potential to subvert the metaphysics both of politics and religion. Yet the incontestable fact that Western societies are built around secular and/or liberal institutions does not automatically mean that the practices of these institutions – as oppressive as Asad and Mahmood describe them – are the exclusive terrain for discussion of the secular.

Even though my purpose here is not to defend liberalism or the empire, I repeat Gourgouris's most significant question in the discussion: *why should a critique of imperialism be framed in antisecularist terms?*[12] Is there historical evidence that makes us ally the oppressive regime of colonial empires with secular imagination? What if the secular works against the empire precisely in the historical appropriations and developments initiated in the oeuvres of these new Muslim intellectuals, whose commitments I find outrageously belittled in simplistic equation with the bureaucrats from the Rand Corporation? After all, the most important point of critical Islam is that any hegemony – no matter whether phrased in the ahistorical terms of subjective autonomy (the secularist subject) or in the ahistorical notions of religious heteronomy (religious alterity) – is subject to time and therefore open to modification, failures, and abolitions. This point is precisely what empowers Islam as agency inside Western discursive frameworks – literally as compatible with the West and not as its eternal and unknowable enemy. Because Islam is in time (via the people who form the confessional and cultural community), it can engage with other peoples' histories, it can change, or it can critique – starting with its own theology – any power claim, including the power of the colonizer, the empire, or the hegemony.

The misreading, on the part of Mahmood, of the intellectual pledge of critical Islam – namely the fact that these new Muslim intellectuals are motivated by the denial of the empire and not by its political support – contributes to a suspicious intertwining of polemics against the Rand report's ideology with the voices of Nasr Abu Zayd, Abdel Karim Soroush, and Hassan Hanafi, quoted by Mahmood as exemplary scholars in the field of Quranic hermeneutics (and targets of Mahmood's attack). While the report, according to Mahmood, suggests that "the recalcitrant Muslim is faulted for his inability to recognize that the truth of Quranic scripture is grounded not in its theological claims but in culture and history . . . some contemporary Muslim reformers . . . exemplify the interpretative stance advocated by the Rand Report."[13] Mahmood continues: "Echoing the Rand Report's contention that the Qur'an is a human rather than divine text, Abu Zayd argues that the Qur'an, once revealed to Muhammad entered history."[14]

It is an interesting question as to why the suggestion that the Qur'an is a human artefact is so scandalous and presumably loaded with the "politics of the enemy" for Saba Mahmood. In what other way does a divine scripture acquire its sacredness if not through the agreement of a certain community of people, which exist – the community and the agreement – in history? It is certainly not up to the Rand Corporation to tell us that the Qur'an is a human text revealed in human language but the hasty alliance of the bureaucratic rhetoric of empire with the life-time intellectual projects of Soroush, Hanafi, and Abu Zayd sounds like a hasty application of the well-known orientalist critique. One of the dangers of the over-exploitation of Said's orientalist thesis is falling victim to the "clichés of orientalism": the inability of postcolonial scholarship to transcend the essentialisms that come out of the dialectics between the East and the West, the civilized and the savage, between religion and secularism, and colonizer and colonized, and to treat them as heterogeneous and internally dynamic terms existing in complicated and changing relationships. This attention to the heterogeneity of the terms is not simply motivated by alliances with the politics of the strong of the day but is entirely for the sake of discovering common sites of existence and dialogue that will bring this community(ies), broken by traumatic memories and past violence, into the future. The Western-Islamic public sphere, via the work of the new Muslim intellectuals, is a perspective pertinent to the new theoretical and social mediations required for overcoming the sterile binaries that classical orientalism mobilizes but does not transcend. The Western-Islamic public sphere, actually, historicizes the polar terms and projects their new meanings and entanglements into the future.

With regard to critical Islam, the reduction of its stakes to the ideological formulas of the Rand report is dangerous (not least) because it does not care about the details and commitments of the intellectual work in question. More important, the attack against these 'liberal' Muslim intellectuals uncritically presupposes – though without outspoken admission – that nonsecular forms of Islam should be empowered as more 'authentic insights' into this radically different (from the Western pole) religion. If Saba Mahmood, Talal Asad, and other postcolonial scholars are indeed so concerned about the normative content of the secular, which, they suppose, is forcefully imposed on Muslim populations through the US imperialistic machine, what is exactly their engagement with the normative impetus of nonsecular Islam? There is no problematization whatsoever, neither in Saba Mahmood's article discussed here nor in the most prominent texts of Asad, of the question of what is Islam if it is not the trope, the religion, the practice, or the civilization that is "created" by the gaze of the Westerner. If the Westerner's views of Islam are discredited as imperialist, if 'Westernized' Muslims' interpretations of Islam are equally discredited as serving foreign agendas, where and who precisely is the authority capable of revealing and judging Islam in a fair and legitimate way? And, even more important, whose voice should the Western publics hear when they try to receive an educated insight into that religion? If I attempt to find the answer in Saba Mahmood's anthropological study exploring the female support for fundamentalist Islam in Egypt, I am left with the following conclusion: active social agents can freely choose patriarchal forms of oppression and through their agency transform the oppression itself into a meaningful lifeworld invested with ethical messages of piety. Therefore, what matters is not that the female mosque movement supports a particular reading of Islam that, by default, deprives women of agency and exploits Islam as a political doctrine, but the fact that the female subject can nonetheless recognize in this structural unfreedom the conditions of its own – I should add illusionary – liberation.[15] Again, obviously for Saba Mahmood, the people who live inside the metaphysical framework of religion, as fanatic, oppressive, patriarchal, and hopeless as it could seem to the outside observer, should be empowered to speak for Islam and not those who have spent their whole life researching the convoluted – social, poetic, cultural – histories of the Islamic civilization; even the various types of feminists – Muslim, Christian, Jewish, and atheist (to name a few), belonging to the whole political spectrum in Egypt – who might have a point to make on female liberation issues should not be listened to. What is more, the argument in *Politics of Piety* obviously suggests that female support for fundamentalism is an expression, somehow, of a more authentic freedom – certainly if researched and understood in its own vernacular grammar – than scholarly opinion, which is always discredited by external political alliances. Respecting deeply the agents of the anthropological terrain that Mahmood has chosen and admiring the careful field-work she has done, I still cannot help but inquire into the politics and fairness of her conclusions.

Eager to disclaim the normative *theology of the secular*, Mahmood ends up defending the normative *theology of the religious* without further self-reflexive problematization. There is a certain unwill-ingness of Mahmood's texts, analyzed here, to admit that, after all, because Islam is a complicated system of significations it is *in history*. Mahmood agrees that women can choose to obey religious and oppressive obligations – that the veil itself is a religious obliga-tion – considered to be revealed by divine authority. However, what is the language of the divine and who are the worldly ones who speak it? The question that Quranic hermeneutics and other critical Muslims ask is actually what mechanisms of authorization (symbols, signs, and communal rules) execute this supposedly otherworldly demand on Earth. In short, politics is something that bears historical dynamics and it requires modes of significations that are human, communal, and thoroughly secular. The veil, therefore, is not just a divine prescription (and why should a divine prescrip-tion have a privileged status over a non-divine prescription) but a system of meanings which is related to the social structure – in the beginning of Islam, as well as in its historical glories and crisis, and today.

The Tyranny of Guilt – A Counterresponse

The other extreme seems to be occupied by thinkers who profess solidarity with an anti-Islamic attitude that Pascal Bruckner provocatively discussed in a series of articles that stirred the schol-arly and public attention in Europe initially in 2007. The debates continue to this day. The 2010 translation in English of Bruckner's 2006 book *La tyrannie de la pénitence: essai sur le masochisme* provoked me "to imagine" Bruckner in dialogue with the North-American postcolonial school represented by Mahmood and Asad. With regard to the orientalist issue and the vehement postcolonial rhetoric against Western liberal principles, Bruckner is implacably politically incorrect:

> What did the crowd of young people shout to Jacques Chirac in 2004, during the first visit of a French president to Algeria since decolonization? "Visas, visas". A malicious wit might say: they drove us out and now they all want to come live with us! That does not cast doubt on the legitimacy of their independence but it does explain this disturbing truth: Europe got over the loss of its colonies much more quickly than the colonies got over their loss of Europe.[16]

The sufferings of the poor and the oppressed under the disciplinary mission *civilisatrice* of the Western colonizer have long been on the European intellectual agenda. While postcolonial scholars today, following the brilliant analysis of Said's concept of orientalism, constantly try to rediscover the topoi of oppression in the bureaucratic and intellectual apparatuses of past and present Western empires (which undoubtedly exist and operate), Bruckner maintains that Europe has generated in parallel a long list of political clichés (traditionally left-wing) about the nobility, moral purity, and worldly superiority of the sufferers. *The Tears of the White Man: Compassion as Contempt* is Bruckner's first book on the topic of guilt expressed in Western intellectual attitudes vis-à-vis the "third world." "Third worldism," therefore, for Bruckner is a 1980s Western sentimental discourse conveying the ridiculous incapability of Western intellectuals to recognize faraway people in faraway places just as normal human beings. Instead, obsessed with the sentimentalism of the reverie, Westerners pictured the other as always spiritually uplifted, free of materialistic desires, sensuous and intuitive rather than rational and analytic, either sexually excessive or indifferent to sexuality, sagacious yet independent from the cold rigidity of Western mind, materially pitiful but morally admirable.[17] The most miserable, the poorest, and the most deprived beings in the far away, exotic regions of the world, Bruckner insists, seemed to the Western eye loftier, more sublime, more authentic, and better than anyone else. Precisely these fantasies, nourished by the romantic eighteenth-century concept of the noble savage, not only doubled the abominable stereotypes of imperialism, this time in the form of admiration rather than hostility, but were, in essence, cryptonormative: racist in fact, these prejudices actually camouflaged the contempt as compassion.[18] These substitutions happened because, obviously, the intellectuals of Europe felt guilty for the assaults of European imperialism and one way to compensate for past atrocities was through the invention of a new dogma: one that glorifies the exotic and that bounds the West to the dubious repentance that brings with itself the unexplainable pleasures of self-hatred. Only the utopia of the spiritually and morally superior ex-colonized populations could redeem the guilt that Europe bore, coupling it with the projections that the former victims might be able to produce better societies. The more intimate and lachrymose the repentance, the more intense and satisfying the pleasure of loathing oneself. "Nothing is more Western than hatred for the West, that passion for cursing and lacerating ourselves. . . . The critical spirit rises up against itself and consumes its form. But instead of coming out of this process greater and purified, it devours itself in a kind of self-cannibalism and takes a morose pleasure in annihilating itself."[19]

The discourse of the noble savage disappeared with the collapse of another utopia, communism, in 1989. Even though today no one longs for distant, exotic, and poor parts of the world, the ideological dreaming of the third-worldist intellectuals has metamorphosed in discourses that describe globalization as a new type of imperialism – oppressive, materialist, consumerist, and ethically detestable – which should be denounced because today, as in the past, the West's success manufactures other peoples' suffering. Certainly, Western wealth and prosperity are productive of everyone else's miserableness and therefore the West, again, deserves the experience – in language, in politics, and in the lifeworld – of guilt. Bruckner is particularly indignant of the intellectual community, which in the elaboration of newer and more complicated multiculturalist theories, in the various public gestures of humility and self-flagellation, has come to resemble a "penitential caste," a "medieval clergy" in the language of Paul Berman (journalist and editor of *New Republic* and one of Bruckner's North-American intellectual mates), not capable of abandoning the semi-clinical swamp of relativism and unredeemable guilt.[20]

The Tyranny of Guilt is a continuation of Bruckner's reflection on the role that European intellectuals play today in proselytizing Western penitence in the post-9/11 world. He is amazed and dismayed by famous and influential figures in the French academia, like Oliver Roy for example (the famous Islamologue), who have been blind to the dangers of radical Islam. Instead, they, following the inertia of the well-known orientalist fascination with "exoticism," continue even today to recognize in religious fanaticism the magnetic, spiritualistic, and charismatic attributes of the other without the least alarm. Roy, having wrongly predicted the failure of political Islam in the Middle East, now attributes every aggression on the part of Western Muslims – from the Rushdie affair, to the *hijab,* or Danish cartoons – to institutionalized Islamophobia and "rejection of immigration"; worse, for Bruckner, these Western *experts* employ their public influence to advocate political relativism:

> Taught for half a century to respect difference, we are asked to avoid evaluating a foreign religion in terms of our Occidental criteria. Cultural relativism commands us to see what we call our values as simple prejudices, the beliefs of a particular tribe called the West. The religion of the Prophet is thus draped in the mantle of the outcast in order to spare it the slightest attack.[21]

Olivier Roy is not the only one who is under Bruckner's attacks. Vincent Geisser – another French professor in Islam – has legitimized the term "Islamophobia" in an authoritative study on France's past and current interactions with the religion. Tracking down journalists, imams, and politicians who have assaulted Islam publicly, Geisser speaks of "Arab Muslim humiliation," which, in Bruckner's interpretation, means, similarly to "Islamophobia," that the West is politely advised by the Western experts in the field to give up the Western way of life and Western values. And, Bruckner's outraged response is again quite condemning:

> We are not going to confine women to the home, cover their heads, lengthen their skirts, or beat up gay people, prohibit alcohol, censure film, theatre, and literature, and codify tolerance in order to respect the overly sensitive whims of a few sanctimonious persons. . . . Islam is part of the French and European landscape, and as such it has a right to freedom of religion, proper places of worship, and respect – on the condition that it itself respects republican, secular rules and do not claim extraterritorial status, special rights, exemption from swimming pools and gymnastics for women, separate education, and various favours and privileges.[22]

Pascal Bruckner finds a particularly inspiring case for his point in the controversial reception of Ayaan Hirsi Ali's ideas and activism.

The Somali-Dutch, former member of the Dutch parliament, and collaborator with Theo Van Gogh (the Dutch director stabbed to death by a Moroccan-Dutch fundamentalist in 2004 for the making of the movie *Submission*, particularly critical towards the Islamic treatment of women) was attacked in a series of publications in *New York Review of Books* for her "slightly simplistic" Enlightenment fundamentalism, by Ian Buruma and Timothy Garton Ash.[23] Criticizing Ayaan Hirsi Ali for her outspoken admiration for the West (evident in Hirsi's Ali's autobiography *Infidel*, in her feminist work *The Caged Virgin: An Emancipation Proclamation for Women and Islam, Nomad* and in her most recent book *Heretic*), Buruma and Garton Ash identify in her work the shallow adoption of Voltaire's mottos from an exotic beauty of mediocre intellect; Buruma and Garton Ash compete to condemn Hirsi Ali's understanding of Islam and to promote the voice of Tariq Ramadan as alternative and more authoritative. Buruma has written a book, *Murder in Amsterdam*, on the Dutch version of multiculturalism in which he is annoyed by and mocks Ali's reading of the Qur'an. Timothy Garton Ash, even more critical himself vis-à-vis Hirsi Ali, is an admirer of both Buruma's conclusions and Ramadan's alternatives.

In an epilogue-like article to *The Tyranny of Guilt*, called "Enlightenment fundamentalism or the racism of the anti-racists," Bruckner is at the peak of his straightforward style of rhythmic irony and flashy yet well-informed accusations against these Western intellectuals enjoying much public credit: Timothy Garton Ash is an honoured British historian and journalist, particularly interested in the past of Central and Eastern Europe, in dictatorships and revolutions; Ian Buruma is a Dutch-British writer and academic, a global authority on issues of human rights, freedom of speech, and democracy. From Bruckner's perspective, Buruma and Garton Ash, blinded by multiculturalist clichés of relativism, have reduced the greatest achievement of Western civilization, namely the Enlightenment, to a bunch of reified prejudices, equal to or worse than other prejudices. It is a well-known fact that Muhammad Bouyeri, the murderer of Theo Van Gogh, is a fundamentalist. For Buruma and Garton Ash, Ayaan Hirsi Ali is no less fundamentalist than Bouyeri because she preaches the same type of fanaticism yet in a subverted form: the Western Enlightenment. This, Bruckner claims, is not only a preposterous comparison but also a sign that, hidden behind a confusing agenda, two well-respected English-speaking intellectuals are not capable of distinguishing a murderer from a rational debater:

> The difference between her and Muhammad Bouyeri, the killer of Theo Van Gogh is that she never advocated murder to further her ideas. "The Koran is the work of man not of God", she writes. "Consequently we should feel free to interpret and adapt it to modern times, rather than bending over backwards to live as the first believers did in a distant terrible time". One searches this sentence in vain for the least hint of sectarianism. . . . But in the eyes of our genteel professors, Ayaan Hirsi Ali . . . has committed an unpardonable offense: she has taken democratic principles seriously.[24]

"The racism of the anti-racists," therefore, for Bruckner is a type of behaviour that, under the pretext of fighting for the voices and rights of the oppressed, denies the right of other people (Ayaan Hirsi Ali is an exemplary victim for this type of attitude because she is a former Somali dissident, a truly abused person who suffered female circumcision and escaped a forced marriage) to express disagreement phrased in the enlightened grammar of the Europeans. Timothy Garton Ash and Ian Buruma are famous for their involvement in anti-racist causes and yet, in their public engagement and acute critique against Ayaan Hirsi Ali, they failed to recognize the real victim as an equal interlocutor who deserves to be treated with dignity. Here is the quote from Timothy Garton Ash that Bruckner majestically ridicules:

> For Garton Ash Ayaan Hirsi Ali "is irresistible copy for journalists, being a tall, strikingly beautiful, exotic, brave, outspoken woman with a remarkable life-story, now living under permanent threat of being slaughtered like Van Gogh." . . . It is no disrespect to Ms. Ali to suggest that if she had been short, squat and squinting, her story and views might not be so closely attended to.[25]

Demeaning Ayaan Hirsi Ali, treating her with machist condescension, belittling her engagement with Islam, Timothy Garton Ash and Ian Buruma – the renowned Western militants for freedom, the defenders of the East Block dissidents of the past – have reduced, Bruckner tells us, a whole class of people, similarly minded to Ali, and their values to buffoonery and prejudice:

> It's not enough that Ayaan Hirsi Ali has to live like a recluse, threatened with having her throat slit by radicals and surrounded by bodyguards. She . . . has to endure the ridicule of the high-minded idealists and armchair philosophers. She has even been called a Nazi in the Netherlands. Thus the defenders of liberty are styled as fascist while the fanatics are portrayed as victims![26]

I would like to mention that Pascal Bruckner's position gained the support of a wide-range of European intellectuals: experts in multiculturalism, scholars in Islam and humanities, Muslim feminists. Necla Kelek, Bassam Tibi, Ulrike Ackermann, Paul Cliterur, among others, participated in the lively debate which *Signandsight* hosted with generosity, in support of Bruckner, while Ian Buruma, Timothy Garton Ash, Halleh Ghorashi, Adam Krzeminski, and Jesco Delrome, among others, have joined voices to defend vehemently the philosophy and politics of multiculturalism in the light of Islamic demands. All their posts are available at the Signandsight.com.

It is interesting to imagine Pascal Bruckner and Saba Mahmood in dialogue. The Pakistani-American feminist scholar, indignant of Western imperialism (synonymous with secularism and American liberalism, especially under the Bush administration), is, among other things very critical of the French *laïcité*:

> the recent French law banning the display of religious symbols (particularly the veil) in public schools may be taken as another example of how a self-avowed secular state has come to define what religious and non-religious attire is in the public domain (something normatively considered a matter of personal choice within liberalism).[27]

Indeed, liberalism has distorted its historical principle of 'tolerance' into secularist imperatives that aim to control – similarly to fundamentalist religion – every last corner of the public sphere, to discipline and to civilize in accordance with a pre-established, socially engineered set of Enlightenment values. To impose this secularist normativity on Islam, Mahmood insists, is a large-scale Western imperialist project that is discursively legitimized through the intellectual critique of secular Islamic hermeneutics. I can only imagine Saba Mahmood's dismay at former Muslims, such as Ayaan Hirsi Ali, supported by people like Pascal Bruckner, who have only suspicions – one on the top of the other – to raise against the dogma, the practice, and the politics of Islam that the West seems, from their perspectives, to welcome uncritically. Bruckner and Hirsi Ali would argue that the empire has yielded to a multiculturalism that has metamorphosed from a political liberal doctrine of the peaceful cohabitation of populations of different ethnic, religious, and cultural background into a discursive hegemony that legitimizes the terror of relativism. Contrary to what Mahmood suggests, the empire has turned against itself a long time ago, putting its past in the service of multiculturalist imperatives that, nonetheless, have not lost their racist nature. When it comes to Bruckner and Hirsi Ali, this situation is certainly a threat that has to be handled politically; even worse, the institutionalized politics of relativism brings only negative consequences for the Muslim populations inside Western settings and masks the racism that it so piously commits to disable: "the proponents of multiculturalism lock subsequent generations born in the West into a no-man's land of moral values. What comes packaged in a compassionate language of acceptance is really a cruel form of racism. And it is all the more cruel because it is expressed in sugary words of virtue."[28]

Therefore it is not difficult to imagine the clashing positions of these two distinct ways of reasoning. On the one hand, we have the postcolonial academic school in North America, according to which the Orient, Islam, the Third World – in this, simplistically named here Mahmoodian line of argumentation – are all Western-invented terms that designate an infantile space, which is terrorized, modified, and subject to various strategies of subjectivization (as if incapable to generate a response) by the empire.

On the other hand, the rhetoric of the hegemony has deeply penetrated Pascal Bruckner's narrative. The French revolution, for Bruckner, generated the discourse and practice of liberty universally shared throughout the West, regardless of political, social, cultural, or historical distinctions. These Enlightenment values have survived all historical crises that questioned the wholeness and legitimacy of the West, which means that they have, historically, proved stronger than all the ideologies that sought to instrumentalize or question them. Indeed, the West – in this Brucknerian line of argumentation

– is one enormous enlightened totality, which must counteract to the threats coming from Islam.

I would not like to deny the efforts of historicization to Mahmood nor to Bruckner. Mahmood questions liberalism in its political interpretation in the United States in the post-9/11 world and she is sceptical vis-à-vis the French *laïcité* as mobilized in the *hijab affair*. Bruckner, on the other hand, suggests a bridge between Europe and the United States that, in a sense, means he is prepared to recognize America as the noble heir of the pure, saintly, and sacred principles of the French revolution:

> We have to bring the two confused parts of the West [America and Europe] because . . . they are the only guarantees of pluralistic political systems. And what do we care about the semantic quarrels over the meaning of "the West", whether there is one West or several, whether we should abandon the term or not, provided that the West remains a subversive principle that challenges traditions and arbitrary power, promotes freedom, and forbids each nation to turn inward on itself (that is why "Western values" are now execrated by all kinds of fanaticism). . . . Reconciling Europe with history and the United States with the world – that is our task at the beginning of the twenty-first century.[29]

Indeed, Bruckner's call is for a new Western universalism that re-invents in new Euro-American political formulas the dialectics that will ground the new communal projects of the West.

And yet Bruckner's and Mahmood's positions seem strikingly similar because they both ignore the opportunities of something I find central in their arguments: the role of intellectuals in designing a model of public connection that is historical and secular – open to modifications and to the future – based on critique and self-interrogation yet not disrespectful of religion. Precisely this perspective, productive of its own relativization and alteration – neither locked in the lure of the rationalistic Kantian autonomy nor obedient to the sterile prescriptions of the absolute and heteronomous Other – I believe, is what makes the Western-Islamic public sphere a qualitatively different angle of engagement.

Critical Perspective – Part II

While I can understand Saba Mahmood's suspicion towards the hermeneutic enterprise (critical Muslim reformers would generate secular formulas of liberation not internal to religious forms of subjectivization), I would like to evoke, in response, a most simple and indisputable fact: every community is organized around certain affectual, i.e. normative, relations no matter if the foundational reference is divine (the God or Gods) or human (the individual or the collective). It is a romantic belief that in the twenty-first century there might be a society – and if there is one, it certainly is not in the Middle East – that could remain untouched and unchanged by forms of secular modernity that are mobilized, today, through technology and the consumer market but which have been prepared in the past by colonial legal rules and educational structures. Even if the accusation against Quranic hermeneutics were legitimate (that it blindingly advocates secularism for Islamic non-secular societies), the suggestion that there is an Islam that – pure, authentic, and non-susceptible to secularization – is omnipresent somewhere in the Orient seems to me somewhat unfair. Even if one turns to Mahmood's ethnography *Politics of Piety*, her argument in support of a feminist perspective that radically adopts the extreme of religion is developed on the study of a limited group of women in three different mosques in Cairo. Authentic as it is, complicated as it might be, this is not the voice of all Muslim people – women or men – in Cairo, let alone in Egypt or in the Muslim world. And even though these women live in a community entirely regulated by the normative tenets of Islam, this community is still a fragment of the heterogeneous, extremely diverse, and resistant to generalization mosaic of the Islamic social *telos*. To put it bluntly, Quranic hermeneutics cannot invent secularization or secularism for Islam because Islamic social practices and histories have been exposed to and profoundly scarred by these processes, actually, since the time of colonization. Institutional secularization in the Muslim world has its own dynamics and it is certainly not a process that has entered the world of Islam without a complicated reaction on the part of the colonized. Quranic hermeneutics, therefore, is not an advocate of secularization or secularism but rather a product of a multilayered and multi-faceted process of exchange and debate. While, for Saba Mahmood, it is important to identify who these critical Islamic figures target as their audience – and she suggests that their addressee is the Islamic world – the perspective of the Western-Islamic public sphere takes into account critical Islam's de-stabilized message and explores how these people engage in the interactions of Islam with the West.

With respect to the concerns that Bruckner vividly pictures, I can pursue the argument in the opposite direction. It is unfair to suggest that Islam cannot be one religion among others, impenetrable, violent, and divorced from Western values; we do not even need critical Islam to tell us this. This is clear in France where the Islamic social network of civil activism is extremely popular and a number of civil Muslim organizations have gained wide and popular recognition by the public authorities. Fadela Amara, Muslim feminist and former president of one of these Muslim organizations, even occupied a very high political position in the government of Francois Fillon. Appealing as it might be, well-grounded, and genuinely alarmed, the position of Bruckner somehow suggests that Muslims will either have to adopt Voltaire or be condemned to ignorance and barbarism. His argument – protective of Ayaan Hirsi Ali – remains nonetheless deaf to other voices prone to subtlety and nuance without the outright denunciation of religion. Colonization is, again, a complicated process and, if Bruckner was truly concerned with its dynamics, he would be able to appreciate that for generations of Muslim thinkers the contact with France has been a positive resource, not only a stigma. Actually, the fact that the colonization was a successfully accomplished project is evident in the feeble scream for legitimacy that critical Islam demands. Sophisticated knowledge of Western analytical tools and cognitive strategies, rich imagery, coherent argumentation, perfect fluency in the language of the colonizer, is what characterizes critical Islam. And yet, to Bruckner's distaste probably, a subtle suspicion exists towards the universality of the ideals of the French revolution. Sympathetic to his critique against Western intellectual circles, I would, nonetheless, suggest that the fact that "armchair philosophers" have not been able to identify critical Islam as interlocutor (and Ayaan Hirsi Ali does not even belong to this circle) does not necessarily mean that it does not exist or that the intellectual work is flawed per se by abstract and reality-divorced formulations. From my perspective, intellectuals should be given a bit more credit in both Mahmood's and Bruckner's critiques.

Certainly, the secularization of scripture as initiated by Quranic hermeneutics or by the projects of Ramadan, Chebel, and Benslama is not the only, the most laudable, the most representative, or the *true* voice of Islam either. In the final chapter of the book, I will show, for example, how Western-Muslim literary voices deal with the same questions that the academic discourses of critical Islam engage, however, with the means of literary imagination. What makes me give so much credit to these new Muslim intellectuals is precisely their understanding, which they try to articulate in Islamic terms, that communities are constituted around norms that human beings adopt, negotiate, and modify in the course of history. Religious or secular normativity, in that regard, cannot be circumvented, simply abolished, or forcefully endorsed by properly manufactured ideologies. Rather, in the perspective of these new Muslims, religion and secularity can be historicized and thus exposed through critique to the limitations of the affectual structures that motivate them. Only an educated framework sensitive to these Western-Islamic convolutions and imbrications can generate non-violent perspectives for multiple yet shared lifeworlds. This is fundamental for the emergence of a Western-Islamic public sphere.

4

Literary Voices Turned Political

In a gripping image deployed in Surah 7, the Qur'an depicts the people who on the Day of Judgment will inhabit the dividing line between heaven and hell and who will be able to converse with the dwellers of both sides (Qur'an, 7: 46–49). The Qur'an is vague on the ultimate destiny of those "people on the edge" even though their whole description is compassionate and one might assume that, in the linear scheme of a sacred text that assigns either salvation or damnation, they will end up on the safer side of the divide. Certainly one might wonder who those people are and draw out of the guesses different projections – probably the Islamic minorities in the West in the uncertain post 9/11 era, those who abandoned or questioned Islam and repented afterwards, those who erred and confessed their errors? Yet those people could very likely be the Muslim intellectuals (who possess all of the above features) – those whom I call pioneers of critical Islam – who are capable of abandoning dogmatic Islam for the sake of re-evaluating the Islamic tradition, and who are, simultaneously, committed to Islam's preservation through critique and secularization.

The critique and secularization of the dogma are important not for the sake of better accommodating Islam in a Western, presumably secularist environment (even though my argument, indeed, is that without both critique and secularization the Western-Islamic public sphere is impossible); they are important not because they advocate the tailoring of Islam in a critical fashion external to Islam and imposed by foreign powers mostly for the sake of colonization – and this is the sin of which Islamic apologists would accuse critical Islam *ad nauseum*. Rather – and this is the core of critical Islam despite all the controversies surrounding its reception – a critique that is always immanently secular (because it does not rely for authorization on transcendental Reason nor on transcendental God) is crucial to any intellectual project, and Islam is not an exception, because such a critique has the capacity to transform and confront seemingly unalterable and inalienable truths. The process of transformation is also one of poiesis where, as a result, otherness is brought to affect the world instead of being received as an exterior authority of submission.

Critical Muslim intellectuals – despite their national, confessional, or intellectual differences – in the context of the Western-Islamic public sphere are the complete opposite of this Taliban spokesman in Afghanistan who in an interview for the Arabic daily newspaper *Asharq Al-Awsat*, published in London, described Islam in the following way:

> Islam is a totality – everything in it is governed by divine law contained in the Holy Book and the prophetic tradition. Everything is included: political, military, economic, social, intimate, legal and ethical matters. Our religion is all-encompassing. We do not need anyone, and especially not the West, in order to complete the sphere that envelopes us. We will only use two externalities; science and technology, to be able to populate such a sphere of material goods that we will provide the exploitation of our natural resources.[1]

Instead, the position that is more or less intrinsic to the agency of critical Islam is well demonstrated in Nasr Abu Zayd's stance on the contextualization of Islam's Holy Book:

> For Muslim scholars, the Qur'an was always a text from the moment of its canonization until the present moment. Yet, if we pay close attention to the Qur'an as a discourse or discourses, it is no longer sufficient to re-contextualize one or more passages in the fight against literalism and fundamentalism, or against a specific historical practice that seems inappropriate for our modern context. Similarly, it is not enough to invoke modern hermeneutics to justify the historicity and hence relativity of every mode of understanding, while in the meantime claiming that our modern interpretation is more appropriate and more valid. Without re-thinking the Qur'an and without re-invoking its living status as a reformation of Islamic thought "discourse", whether in academia or in everyday life, democratic and open hermeneutics cannot be achieved. . . . To reconnect the question of the meaning of the Qur'an to that of the meaning of life, it is now imperative to note that the Qur'an was the outcome of dialogue, debate, augment, acceptance and rejection, both with pre-

Islamic norms, practices and culture, and with its own previous assessments, presuppositions and assertions.[2]

However, the Muslim intellectuals inside the Western-Islamic public sphere are not only scholars of the Qur'an but also, as mentioned in the introduction, all kinds of public figures who utilize critique in order to initiate dialogue with the dogma – regardless of whether their interest is focused on the classical dogmatic corpora as in the case of Quranic hermeneutics or on other forms of local or popular Islam. I am not interested in classifying those Muslim intellectuals according to complex topographies that measure the extent of their religiosity or moderation, their legitimacy or pathos as reformers, the extent to which they adopt "modernity" or stay locked inside the tradition. There is currently one such comprehensive study on Western Islamic intellectual discourse, which, I believe, has achieved everything in the aspect of classification without, however, discussing in depth any of the ideas and dilemmas that come with critical Islam.[3] What is important for me, as far as the Western-Islamic public sphere is concerned, is the operation of critique as the primary agent in the production of religious knowledge that contributes to the shaping of an open critical space, which is always in-the-making, always open to change, rather than firmly established and closed. Precisely the critical potential of dialogue itself is the cipher for understanding the somehow escaping meaning of the transformation that the Western-Islamic public sphere presupposes and, hopefully, brings.

Among the many names of active Muslim intellectuals in both Europe and North America (and here one should pay due respects to such gigantic and controversial reformers as the UCLA professor Khaled Abou El-Fadl; to the American-born Islamic feminist and the first female Imam in the contemporary history of Islam, Amina Wadud; to the moderate and interesting professor Muqtedar Khan from the University of Maryland; to Reza Aslan, who is a controversial scholar of Islam, a reformer, and an activist; to Osama Siblani, who since 1984 has edited the influential newspaper *Arab-American News* and who is simultaneously an American patriot, a pious Shiite, and a radicalized supporter of Hezbollah; and the list goes on) I have chosen to discuss here four literary figures, quite different from each other, whose work and public activity has not yet significantly captured the attention of current Islamic scholarship. They are the French-Arab intellectual Abdelwahab Meddeb, two young novelists of Pakistani origin, Ali Eteraz and Nadeem Aslam, and Orhan Pamuk, the Turkish Nobel Prize laureate for literature for 2006.

Abdelwahab Meddeb – distinguished French literary figure of Tunisian origin, winner of several prestigious prizes [Francois Mauriac (2002), Max Jacob (2002), and Benjamin Fondane (2007) for literature in France], cultural critic and professor of Comparative Literature at the University of Paris X-Nanterre – is one of the most conspicuous public opponents to the kind of theology – which Meddeb does not hesitate to term as "fundamentalist" and "fascist" – that Tariq Ramadan advocates. On January 30, 2008, Meddeb even engaged in a public debate with Ramadan, transmitted on France 3, in which issues ranging from Islamic fundamentalism to the presence of Islam in the West were discussed.[4] Certainly, the debate was provoked by the fact that the *hijab affair* in France (at this time with a worldwide resonance) was still a heated public topic and Meddeb, as a passionate critique of the veil, had been recruited as a consultant for the Debré Commission supposed to "save" the French *laïcité* from the militant Islam[5]; but also pertinent was the publication of Meddeb's two books – *Sortir de la Malediction* and *La Maladie d'Islam* – in which the author expressed his profound inquietude about the latest post-9/11 developments in Islam. Meddeb's work, therefore, is important because it shows the tensions existing between some of the academic trends in critical Islam (Tariq Ramadan's controversial thought in particular) and the literary production of critical Islam.

On the other hand, the young novelists – Ali Eteraz and Nadeem Aslam – are important because the manner of their self-styling appeals to young people, well versed in the new media technologies and the global publics. Eteraz and Aslam enjoy less attention from the traditional media, yet they are addressed by online media and are present on blogs, in literary and youth magazines, etc.; they do not speak from the position of the highest authority of Islam – as qualified imams – and they do not label portions of Islam as "right" or "wrong" but rather write from within the Islamic texts and from within personal experiences of Islam that pertain more to the actual praxis of religion than to its unmovable ethical layer; they do not attempt to be politically correct in order to please the various audiences exposed to their messages and certainly they do not aim at immediate political gains in the game with the highest stakes between *Islam* and the *West*. However, both Ali Eteraz and Nadeem

Aslam are Pakistani-born novelists, residing respectively in the United States and England, who speak in the quiet, sympathetic, yet vociferous voice of insiders as they depict the physical and psychological violence committed in the name of God. What actually unites Eteraz's and Aslam's intellectual efforts is a particular, both artistic and political, reaction to 9/11. The events on the 9/11 provide an opportunity for a self-interrogatory journey to the depths of their own religion and culture and an inquiry into its historical, political, and everyday intertwinements with the West. The result is a memoir – *Children of Dust* – which describes Ali Eteraz's coming to America's Bible Belt (Alabama) from a fundamentalist religious school in Pakistan and his subsequent voyage from religion to fundamentalism and from there to atheism and back to religious reformation; Aslam's *Maps for Lost Lovers* is a quasi-autobiographical novel dedicated to 9/11 (even though its fictional setting is Britain in 1997), whose absent protagonists, Chanda and Jugnu, "are the 9/11 of this book in that violence was done to them in the name of religion but it wasn't religion at all but hundreds of different things."[6] Nadeem Aslam, who is in fact a British citizen of immigrant Pakistani origin, is quite straightforward about his engagement with 9/11:

> I read letters from Muslims about how bad things were in New York. And it is bad. But I thought, it would be so refreshing in those letters if you mentioned that before 9/11 you didn't have to go through this, that something happened on 9/11. Can we have please a few sentences condemning Osama bin Laden? People think it's implicit. Why do we have to say it? People say, leave us alone, we are decent people, we are not involved. I sympathised with that viewpoint, but these are strange times. We are involved. They involved us. Let's ask moderate Muslims to stand up and say it.[7]

My final sub-chapter is focused on the concepts of history and religion in Orhan Pamuk's novel *My Name Is Red*. Pamuk is a world-renowned Turkish novelist and one of the only two Muslim Nobel laureates for literature. His work, which as a whole spans more than thirty years now, is important for me (and a commentary of it is intentionally chosen as the end of the whole book) because its topics, politics, and outspoken commitments perfectly embody the aspirations of the literary branch of critical Islam. My interest in Pamuk stems not only from the fact that many of the dilemmas that haunt critical Islam find imaginative translations in his writing but also because his work, especially the novel under discussion here, is one of the artist, understood broadly and beyond the confines of *ars poetica*: as the work of the one who is in possession of the transformative power of the poetical, capable, as Plato's poet, to produce change in the politics and morals of his time.

On the Politics of Literary Texts

It should be, probably, difficult to explain why I would like to present literary writing as one of the foundations – with all the theoretical limitations of the term – of a critical public sphere that has immediate political consequences. Literary art, which is also poetic, in order to be political should be involved in re-inventing, transforming, or re-imagining portions of reality. Imagination and critical thinking are indeed the smallest political denominator for generating a change in what already exists. What is more, the way in which critique operates in literary texts (those of interest here) – and this is fundamental to my concept of a Western-Islamic public sphere – is by simultaneously transcending the limiting confines of Reason (through imagination) and the submissive consolation of Piety (through critical distance from unknowable Absolutes). Political thinking, therefore, is not engaged in acquitting the world of its uncertainty and precariousness but rather it embraces them in the complex process of constituting truth, which is always also the process of creating truth.[8] Therefore, what really makes the Western-Islamic public sphere a political sphere is that freedom and autonomy could be claimed, if not fully achieved, as the most desired form of human experience. In other words, literary voices are political because they are capable of conceiving projects for the celebration of ordinary life in a truly miserable, full of all kinds of fanaticisms, world.[9]

At the same time, I am inherently indebted in my reflection to Davide Panagia's approach in *The Political Life of Sensation,* which aims to identify sensations and sensuous experiences – which could also be poetic experiences – as essentially political.[10] The argument is complex not least because it goes against traditional narratological modes of political deliberation (such as reading and writing) but also because it requires, as Panagia shows, a rethinking via Rancière and Deleuze, of the whole Kantian aesthetics. Despite the fact that

The Political Life of Sensation distances itself from narrative (which, by default, is the work of literary writing), what I borrow from Davide Panagia is the identification of moments of "interruption and reconfiguration that . . . comprise the aesthetic-political dimensions of democratic life."[11] Certainly, the point that Panagia develops pertains to the political substance of visual poetics. Yet, his insight that the precarious, indeterminate, and allusive are radically democratic and political in nature, that, in fact, in the constant transformation, reconfiguration, and mutations of power resides the true 'essence' of democracy is what inspires me to envision the Western-Islamic public sphere as a democratic universe open to constant interrogations and transformations. Taking a slightly different route, though, I would like to identify those radical moments of democracy, which are also poetic, in the complex narratives of the Western Muslim intellectuals.

Abdelwahab Meddeb's Public and Literary Project

Even though Meddeb has never enjoyed such fame as Ramadan, he, similarly to the Swiss scholar, has a solid Islamic background, which, instead of being wrapped in the charismatic allure of the radical and insurgent Muslim Brotherhood,[12] is conventional and old-fashioned: Meddeb's father was a famous scholar in *fiqh* in Tunis while Meddeb himself was trained in one of North Africa's mosque universities, Zitouna, before leaving Tunis for France in 1968. After 9/11, Abdelwahab Meddeb's work was devoutly dedicated to explaining the essence of the "malady of Islam," which for him comes as a result of complex intersections of theological, cultural, and geo-political historical circumstances: While theologically the Islamic subject constitutes itself vis-à-vis Judaism and Christianity through the wound of the excluded orphan (Ishmael), the poetry and music of the classic Islamic civilization has been systematically robbed in history by movements pioneering return to the letter and Quranic purity. The ideologies of Ibn Hanbal (d. 855) and Ibn Taymiyyah (d. 1328), two of the classical legalists of the Medina utopia, the Almoravid and Almohad Berber dynasties, and the Wahhabite movement in the eighteenth century, obsessed with the restoration of the mythic model of Medina, are the inspirational sources of contemporary fundamentalism. Another important nuance is added if one considers the alliance of the United States with Pakistan in the struggle against the Soviet invasion in Afghanistan, when an international brigade of Islamic fighters, well conversant in technology, was financed with Saudi petrodollars. In addition to that, the drama of Palestine nourishes the resentment of Islam in a historical moment when the European colonial influence with its imported idea of secular state is gradually replaced by a type of Americanization that, apart from championing consumerism, technology, and shallow modernisation, advocates a new type of pious hegemony.[13]

Yet none of these is the *truth* of Islam, which, for Meddeb, is to be found in the poetry of Abu Nuwas (762–813) and Ibn Arabi (1165–1240), which praises homosexual love, wine, and spiritualism, the Islam which is in the corporal pleasures exhibited in *One Thousand and One Nights* and in the rationalism of the Arabo-Occidental philosophy of Averroes and Avicenna, the Islam which is in the free thinking of the theosophists and the Sufis, the Islam which is encoded in the atomic beauty of the arabesques and in the secrecy of the Arabic calligraphy, revealing, in addition to the Quranic chant, another locus of encounter between the fallible human and the unknowable God. Today, the chagrin of Meddeb is enormous, instead of capitalizing on these traditions,

the Islamic subject is no longer man of the "yes" that illuminates the world and creates a naturally hegemonic being; from sovereign being he has become a man of the "no", the one who refuses, who is no longer active but only re-active. This sentiment, initially unknown to the Islamic subject, will imperceptibly grow in him and take over his center. I believe that the fundamentalist actions whose center is the Islamic subject can be explained by the growth of the latter's *ressentiment*, a state that has historically been unknown to him since he has come upon the scene of history as subject.[14]

Certainly, fundamentalism in Islam has a scriptural basis, a fact that makes the whole re-interpretation of the textual corpora urgent. At the same time, it must be declared that fundamentalism and fascism in contemporary Islam are incontestable tendencies despite all efforts for *liberation*.

The Quranic letter, if submitted to a literal reading can resonate in the space delimited by the fundamentalist project: it can respond to one who wants to make it talk within the narrowness of those confines; for it to escape, it needs to be invested with the desire of the interpreter. Rather than distinguishing a good Islam from a bad Islam, it would be better for Islam to open itself to debate and discussion, to rediscover the plurality of opinions, to set up a space for disagreement and difference.[15]

However, from Meddeb's standpoint, the deployment of the labels "fascism" and "fundamentalism," if done with delicacy and nuance, offers with regard to Islam a robust and necessary defense. Differentiating between Islam and Islamism (with the latter's adjacent fascistic and fundamentalist branches) is one way of showing that Islam is an ancient, multiple, and polyphonic tradition with a complex and contradictory origin while Islamism is a thoroughly abhorrent and despotic instrumentalization of the old religion.[16] Al-Qaeda, Hamas, Hezbollah, and the Iranian theocrats are fascist for Meddeb because their ideologies not only aim to colonize every small area of private life, but also because they preach extermination of whole sectors of society (the Jews, the apostates, the unfaithful) through simplistic and all-encompassing ideologies.

The argument becomes more complicated when thought through the prism of the Western-Islamic public sphere because it evokes historical entanglement and competition for authoritative opinions. It turns out that Tariq Ramadan's voice is promoted by a whole group of public figures in the West, the journalists Timothy Garton Ash and Ian Buruma, the sociologists Olivier Roy and Armando Salvatore among others, while Abdelwahab Meddeb's message appeals to a different circle: literati, scholars and, most of all, French intellectuals from the Maghreb. Tariq Ramadan's project is inspired by the twelfth-century philosopher Al-Ghazali (d.1111), who, according to Ramadan, anticipated seventeenth-century Descartes.[17] Al-Ghazali articulated a doctrine of a supreme powerful God. This God, experienced through mystical or ecstatic reunion, enslaves man as His regent on Earth, which brings rejection of all natural theology and all independence of human beings from divine will. This is the tradition that fascinates Tariq Ramadan – as declared in his books *Radical Reform and Islam* and *The West and the Challenge of Modernity* – and it also informs much of Ramadan's public commitments.[18]

As far as Meddeb is concerned, this is fundamentalist rhetoric. It has permeated the Western publics in the scandals over the hijab and Salman Rushdie and it is also evident in every single Western debate concerning Islam since 1989: the Theo Van Gogh murder, through the importation of Saudi imams and the cartoon affair in Denmark, through the debates on the introduction of sharia laws and the building of mosques, through demands for Muslim healthcare, etc. One of the propagandists of fundamentalism in the Western setting, Meddeb insists, is Tariq Ramadan. Certainly "fascism" is a strong word and one would wonder why Abdelwahab Meddeb did not choose to give the Islamist doctrine under critique a different name (totalitarianism, theocracy, dictatorship) and here, it seems, is the answer: because fascism evokes the past and speaks directly to the historical memory of the West. What Tariq Ramadan's theology advocates from below its tolerant and multiculturalist surface, in Meddeb's terms, is something the West has already experienced under a different guise – dangerously oppressive ideology and practice which leave humanity in moral and physical devastation, and with long-term incinerating guilt.

Intellectually, Abdelwahab Meddeb's project, which stems from the exploration of the complex relationship between colonizers and colonized, has a politically different tenor from the one of Ramadan. On the one hand, Meddeb's work addresses the ambiguous legitimacy of the francophone literature written by Arab intellectuals and targeting simultaneously the Arab-Islamic audiences and the Western publics, while on the other hand, he affirms that out of the two poles – colonizer versus colonized – there comes a complex in-between which is multilingual, hybrid, autonomous, and fluid, and which can be described with neither of the two terms. This is an intense universe of exchange that writers, like him, who are as much French as Arab, create and inhabit. In the words of Abdel Kabir Khatibi – a French-educated Moroccan literary figure – the major responsibility of French-Arab intellectuals is to articulate a new notion of history that deconstructs the simplistic binaries (civilized-savage, colony-metropolis, religion-secularism) of the colonial period: "Our recent history (personal and national) is inscribed between the power and the letter. If this wound conveys one all too blinding present, it also masks the difficulty, the immense difficulty, of thinking the concept of history."[19] Precisely inside a common Western-Islamic or Western-Arabic in-between the porous and polar historical relationship is evoked as a living and moving space of heterogeneity. From the perspective of this new class of French-Arab postcolonial intellectuals, this common, yet fractured by memories and violence, space neither results from the recent visibility of Islam in Western debates nor is it a consequence of the 9/11 event, but it is a historical space with a more ancient origin. In line with the argument for the emergence of a Western-Islamic public sphere, I would even argue that this space results from complicated historical imbrications that, together with the political oppression and colonial dependence of the Orient, have generated a whole class of Western-educated Muslim intellectuals, fluent and writing in Western languages, and prepared to confront the Western publics from the standpoint of the equal interlocutor. Exploring the different mediums of literature and theology, different in message and appealing to different circles, Meddeb and Ramadan are, in a sense, the perfect representatives of this new class of public figure whose dialogue with history has a political reference to the present. Despite their differences, the political message seems common: "In order to steal the ground from under the menacing eye of the agitated who occupy the political territories of Islam, it would be appropriate to work on rendering Islam interior to Europe. This would adorn it with a dignity that would have the aura of the universal."[20]

Meddeb's literary world is penetrated by something that Dina Al-Kassim terms, very successfully, *calligraphesis* – a neologism that combines the author's tendency for an ornamental expressionistic style and reflections on calligraphy (especially in the novel *Talismano*) with the systematic experimentations and abuses of the grammar and syntax of the classical French language.[21] The very language of Meddeb (which is a whole literary universe in itself), borrowing expressions and themes from the religious Arabic tradition and the Qur'an, from the multiple and dispersed Maghrebi and Berber dialects, from the French literary canon and postmodern experimentalism, was already in the 1980s a political call for rethinking the relationship between language and power. "Writing in French 'surrenders' us to the other, but we will defend ourselves with the arabesque, the subversion, the maze, the labyrinth, the incessant decentering of the sentence and of language so that the other will get lost just as in the narrow streets of the casbah."[22] The French language, when utilized by an Arab intellectual, can never be a mere translation of the oppressed term in the idioms of the oppressor, or vice versa. Rather, it is a conscientious expropriation and a legitimate creative-literary abuse, nourished not only by a transformative impetus but also by the performative desire to express new forms of connection and social critique. Therefore the existence of Arabic calligraphic textuality in Meddeb's novels and

poems within the architectural framework of the French language –
calligraphesis – is a political statement rehabilitating the Orient and
Islam as an internal – rich and equal in dignity – partner to the voice
of the hegemonic colonizer. Through the agency of this hybrid,
literary language is revived the agency of the seemingly silent,
abused, primitive, and speechless (post)colonial subject. Actually,
the experience of the colonized who speaks the language of the colonizer is resistant to any totalization: this subject inhabits a liminal
space between life and death, between compulsion and repetition,
between resistance and submission, between Allah and his denial, a
space that coincides with neither of these extremes but is their exact
broken middle; a space where all the memories of violence and division could be re-articulated in a broken language that connects
rather than divides, right in this in-between, the postcolonial subject
with the former colonizer.

In answer to the question "Pourquoi Écrivez-Vous," asked by
Libération in 1985, Meddeb gives the following convoluted series of
metaphors:

> I write haunted by the hand amputated in my previous life when I
> was a scribe for a Persian vizier. . . . I had invented a style that harmo-
> nizes the form with the number. My jealous master accused me of
> extortion and reported me to the law; this is how my hand was cut
> off. When I returned to life, a thousand years later, I grew up on the
> shores of Africa. While I sojourned under dark skies, I was initiated
> into the mysteries of the western exile. There, I translate from
> memory the voice of the angel which I transcribe in a foreign
> language in order to conjure the atavistic amputation and re-educate
> this hand that moves as intractable graft under the reminiscence of
> the log spattered with my blood after the hit of the executioner,
> which threw me into unconsciousness; an arm which mourns, a
> stump of an orphan hand which knocks, claws, grabs, claws, gives,
> caresses; a hand which when writing gathers in one unique gesture
> all the exchanges that it is capable of.[23]

Writing itself for Meddeb, obsessed with pain and memory, opens
nonetheless a space for their transgression where – "in one unique
gesture" – modernity, tradition, and avant-garde playfulness, the
Orient and the West, exist in aporetical complicity.

The politics of Meddeb's message, indispensable for the
aesthetics of the text/writing, is particularly evident in the novel

Talismano. In a hallucinatory journey back to Tunis, the Westernized protagonist becomes immersed in the enchanted universe of pagan debauchery, sorcerers, exorcists, calligraphers, tattoo artists, the ghoulish mob, the Sufi poetry, the philosophy of Ibn Arabi, and the Text (the Qur'an). The elusive multiplicity of the Orient is also intertwined in a series of imagined interactions with a number of great Western authors: Dante Alighieri, Constantine Cavafy, and Jean Genet. While the narrative hesitates between the Maghreb, Europe, and the Middle East and while the language evokes latinized *bismillahs* (the beginning of the Islamic prayers) and Quranic and psalmic allusions, the final scenes delicately imbricate all the heterogeneous voices and epochs in a single crowd who witnesses in mesmerized hypnosis the carnivalesque ruin of Halfawine, the Tunisian city revisited in reverie. On the one hand, it seems, Meddeb deliberately meets and mirrors heterogeneous discourses inside the narrative of *Talismano* under the assumption that there exists an irreducible difference informing the subjectivization in the colony. On the other hand, the message is no less oriented towards the Western subject who is conceived as a historical witness to, and participant in, the writing of a common social space. In the ruins of Halfawine, out of the dreamy landscape of the Orient and through the medium of the French language, systematically abused in linguistic experiments, dense with Islamic references, and flooded with calligraphic tropes, a new type of social imaginary is born, which is historical, open, hyphenated: Western-Islamic, French-Arab, or secular and religious at the same time.

While the journey is obviously an attempt of the divided subject to come to terms with the plurality of references constitutive of his origin, it is also a gesture of desacralization vis-à-vis the founding scripture. The novelist (he coincides with the narrator), who is the manipulator of the written word, competes with God in the realm of language. "My first quarrel with the father burst in a mixture of words during the transmission of the recited text."[24] In the myriad of references that build the multi-layered texture of the novel, the Qur'an is not evoked as the immutable and only Word of a transcendent and ahistorical Absolute, but rather as a text that can take the offenses of authorial sacrilege. For example, in *Talismano* Meddeb describes the calligraphers as free in their prayers from the traditional constraint to address Allah when chanting or drawing. Rather, they inscribe in the talisman a *Hallajian* motto – a Sufi evocation of God that in writing is marked by a blank space (God is absent) and in the chant is marked by silence (God cannot be spoken). Therefore, in Meddeb's novel God is desacralized as far as he does not lurk behind the lines of an ahistorical scripture. Allah here is an abyss of blankness that acquires historical presence through various articulations in French-Arab and in the playful encounter between piety and blasphemy.

The institution of the sacred text is destabilized, even expropriated, by the artist and subordinated, in a sense, to the *ars poetica* of the exile who transforms and alters the legacies that the Eastern-Western histories have inscribed on him. At the same time, this intellectual rehabilitation of the exile as the carrier of a new type of subjectivity is profoundly embedded in the religious insofar as it is a reminder that Islam begins, *avant la léttre*, with Abraham's and Ishmael's exiled genealogies.

In another novel, *Phantasia*, Meddeb articulates Islam as a tradition that privileges exile – or the identity in-the-making – more than any other stable historical reference. The figure of the exile maintains the bond with the Judeo-Christian narrative and it enriches even further the tradition through the biography of the orphaned Prophet Muhammad.[25] What seems more important for Meddeb, however, is that the trope of exile, if understood in its theological profundity, should prevent the religious tradition from fundamentalist and political instrumentalizations because it subverts the claims over territorial, intellectual, or spiritual patrimony. Yet, in Islam, similarly to the Bible, the relationship between Ishmael and Muhammad is constructed in language; it is linguistic, mythical, and phantasmal from its very beginning. "There is no merit in having this truth furnish its proof in the authenticity of history. This genealogy is a mythology tested by language."[26] While classical theology naturalizes the religious mythos transforming it into the truth of the Absolute, Meddeb's narrator experiences exile as a continuous linguistic conundrum confronting him, endlessly, with the plurality of his origin.

Critical Reception

While Tariq Ramadan's theology has critiques and supporters, the same is true for Abdelwahab Meddeb's thought. Carine Bourget, for example, in an article on Meddeb and Ben Jelloun (another French-Muslim literary figure) directly accuses the two French intellectuals of didactics, of a failure to "present a balanced account of the issues surrounding the headscarf affair in France," in complicity with Western media propaganda after 9/11 and in contribution "to the confusion between Islam and terrorism."[27] Bourget is indignant about the diagnosis that Meddeb gives to the "sickness" of contemporary Islam, namely Islamic fundamentalism. In *The Malady of Islam*, however, Meddeb is particularly clear that fundamentalism is an abominable instrumentalization of the complicated, ancient, and rich religion, a distortion that seeks to restore the letter of Islam but betrays the spirit. Meddeb is extremely straightforward in his own definition of what, for him, is *authentic* Islam. Theologically, it is a creative heir to the rationalist theology of the Mut'azilites and, civilizationally, it is indebted to the artistic developments of the classic Arabic caliphate:

> It was in . . . Baghdad of the first part of the ninth century that the great scientific adventure of Arabic literature began, an adventure that lasted into the sixteenth century. It was at that time that the school of astronomy of Baghdad was created, founded both on speculative calculations and on observation. It was also in that city that algebra was invented by al-Kwarizimi. . . . Besides this scientific movement there was born a poetic revolution reminiscent of the nineteenth-century poetic revolution in France. If the reader can transcend context and history, he or she can hear how the words of these Arab poets resonate with those of Baudelaire, Verlaine, Rimbaud and even Mallarme.[28]

Carine Bourget further stigmatizes Meddeb as "downright orientalist"[29] because in a passage in the book he evokes Flaubert's fascination with Kuchuk Hanem, the oriental belly dancer who nourishes the male fantasies in *Voyage en Orient*. And this accusation (unfortunately, after Said's *Orientalism* any remote comparison between Islam and the West is considered an intentional abuse of Islam) is done without any acknowledgment of the fact that Meddeb's reference is only to say that, from his perspective, there was a time in the past when Islam cultivated a civilization of sensuousness and corporal pleasures: a civilization with special attention to the beauty of the body echoing the famous hadith that says "God is beautiful and loves beauty," a civilization assaulted today by clerics and censors, by "semiliterate people sick with resentment," who, by advocating the veil (especially in its radical black forms), maltreat the female body in the suffocating summer heats, who "abolish the aesthetic dimension that accompanies the ethics of Islam," who make the body disappear, and who, ultimately, have transformed the ancient sites of the Islamic civilization "from paradise into hell."[30] In the same chapter, Meddeb reminds the reader that while medieval Christianity despised the sensuality of the body, Islam from the same period developed a cult for the body which could be observed in the language of *One Thousand and One Nights* and in the theology of Sheikh Nafwazi who praised the body in *The Perfumed Garden*, a cult that could be recognized in the amazement of European literary figures with the oriental artifice (Diderot, Flaubert, Maupassant, among others), and a cult that has penetrated even the Arabic language itself as far as the word for "religious marriage" means also coitus, or sexual pleasure.[31]

Similarly to Sabah Mahmood in her denouncement of Quranic hermeneutics, Carine Bourget is unfairly dismissive of the larger commitments that inform Meddeb's project, and, in a way, even though unconsciously, she is dismissive of this classical Islamic heritage whose restoration and dignity he pursues and defends. Belittling his work as "orientalist" and normatively bound to the French state ideology of *laïcité*, Bourget is insensitive to a voice that comes from within the Islamic social imaginary, which means, ironically, that she herself betrays the anti-orientalist assumption. More importantly, this ardent polemic against Meddeb's and Ben Jelloun's literary and journalistic work, which reduces their erudite multiple and layered engagement with Islam (an engagement born out of the intricacies of the Arab-French historical intertwinements) to simple spokespersons of the French government, annihilates any reflection on the complexities of the secular dimension of history and presupposes instead that another politics – probably one based on transcendental religious commands – is possible. Hasty to denounce Quranic hermeneutics and critical literary analysis as an essentialist approach to Islam, which in Bourget and Mahmood, among others, appears also as "liberalist," "secularist," and "secular," these brilliant North-American scholars work not in favour of the autonomy of the enlightened subject, but, rather in favour of its subverted other: the ahistorical heteronomy of the religious alterity. As already commented in chapter 2 and 3 of the book, both approaches are equally problematic from the standpoint of the Western-Islamic public sphere.

Ali Eteraz's *Children of Dust*

Children of Dust is a memoir by the very young – only 28 years of age when he completed it in 2009 – Pakistani-American journalist, lawyer, blogger, and activist, Ali Eteraz. The title is significant because it contains a reference to a Surah in the Qur'an where Satan declares his lack of respect for the worldly creatures (human beings) that God had created out of dust (Qur'an 17:61). And at the same time the title is in itself a cipher for understanding the political and poetical substance of the whole book: human nature's transitoriness and historicity, just like dust, disappear into the passage of life as a reminder of our immediate and daily mortality. And yet even if the process of human civilization is marked from the outset by elusiveness and ephemerality, this same process is also a paradoxical testimony to the capacity of human beings for invention (of themselves and their others) out of the temporal, despite the transcendental Absolute that had decreed otherwise. If, however, one admits that humans invent the conditions of their own worlds because of the divine sanction (and not against it), then we are presented with a concept of God who is capable of acknowledging and recognizing his own abolition by the intrinsic truths of all other gods that, in the course of history, have questioned the legitimacy of a singular, the one and the only *not god but God*. In either case, what we are left with is the imaginative, secular, perpetually relativized by its own claims, signature of the divine rather than an unknowable and inaccessible God.

At the same time, the title of the memoir is a direct reference to the main character's perpetual search for identity, which inevitably involves coming to terms with Islam, Pakistan, and America. The memoir is split into five parts, in each of which the narrator appears under a different name invented to present the complex anchoring of a person who re-discovers and re-fashions constantly his own self vis-à-vis a whole ensemble of loyalties whose centrifugal center is the Islamic religion. The first part, called "The Promised, Abir Ul Islam" (literally "Perfume of Islam"), narrates a family's hopes that their son would lead a pious life. The father made a covenant with God before Abir's birth: "Ya, Allah! If you should give me a son, I promise that he will become a great leader and servant of Islam."[32] When Abir was born his mother made the *hajj* and rubbed her son's chest at the Ka'ba in Mecca so that Allah would bless him with piety and determination to serve the religion of Islam. And this covenant, indeed, underlies the whole structure of the novel as well as the life of the person described in it.

The childhood of Abir in Pakistan was careless and joyful in the sweet and strict company of his parents and the whole extended family of various grandparents, aunts, uncles, and cousins; in the company of the Qur'an, too, which reached the child through the accounts of his mother yet mixed with fairy tales of Islam and stories about the *Jinn* (Arab. evil spirit) that penetrated ambiguously the real and imaginative worlds of everyday life in Pakistan. After Abir experienced the brutal and extremely abusive education of the local *madrassa* (Arab. Islamic school) consisting of regular beatings and the mindless memorization of one book only, the Holy Qur'an, his father obtained an American visa and the whole family left Pakistan in search of their own American dream in Alabama (or Allahbama, as they settled to call their new home). Here, at an American high school Abir Ul Islam changed his name to Amir as a teenage rebellion against his parents' fundamentalism. Trying to negotiate his own way between the Qur'an Study Circle (organized by his family and other Muslim immigrants who fought to preserve Orthodox Islam and raise their children according to its tenets), the sexualized teenage sitcoms on American television, and the temptations of the chat rooms, Amir decided to liberate himself through enrolment in a Manhattan university. Part three, called "The Fundamentalist: Abu Bakr Ramaq," actually tells the story of Amir's return to Islamic orthodoxy nurtured in the circle of his roommates in New York, pious and highly devoted Muslims. Having discovered that he descended from Abu Bakr Siddiq, the truth-teller, a companion of the Prophet and the first Caliph of Islam, Amir changed his name again, as a tribute to his heritage and growing devotion to Islam, to Abu Bakr Ramaq (Arab. "Spark of light"). Towards the end of book three, this pious descent turned out to be a forgery, invented only to mask the "disgraceful" Hindu origin of (now) Abu Bakr's family.

The new friends of the protagonist in New York do not socialize with people outside the immediate circle of the pious: they neither drink nor go to parties but instead choose the company of the American movies. One movie that was particularly disturbing for Abu Bakr Siddiq – *The Siege* – portrayed, on the one hand, suicide bombers as pious Muslims while, on the other hand, rejected armed violence as a legitimate response in the fight against terrorism:

At the end of the movie I learned that the same confusion extended to the rest of the group. We'd gone expecting to become angry – no, more angry – and we'd left not knowing what to say. Opting for the easy way out, we ignored the big issues and focused on minutiae: we called Tony Shalhoub a sellout for playing an FBI agent and mocked the way the film messed up little stylistic details. "Did you see how the guy doing ablution washed his arms before washing his face?" I said. "Hollywood sucks! Always demonizing Islam!"[33]

In the company of people admiring Osama bin Laden, tormented by loyalty to Islam and doubts about it, after reading Salman Rushdie's *Satanic Verses*, the young protagonist, following the Islamic scholar Zaid Shakir, made up his mind that secularism was profoundly un-Islamic and contaminated by Western rationale. The liberating force of reason was misguiding because it separated the here from the hereafter, the creation from the Creator. The third part ends with Abu Bakr's misfortunate journey back to Pakistan in the search of a pious wife (since none of the American girls that he met seemed appropriate enough for becoming his virtuous Muslim spouse). There he not only discovered his fabricated noble origin but also encountered excessive hostility on the part of his relatives and former friends who saw him as a "stand-in for the entirety of the infidel West. To be more blunt: I was not a part of the ummah, the universal brotherhood of Muslims."[34]

In the fourth part, Abu Bakr adopts a new identity as the title suggests, "The Postmodern – Amir Ul Islam" (Arab. The Prince of Islam). Disappointed with his trip to Pakistan, he chooses to transfer to a Christian university in Atlanta, majoring in Philosophy and Postmodernism. Religion does not abandon him entirely; in a quite cynical way and in pursuit of public acknowledgement and personal gains (such as unlimited sexual freedom), he instrumentalizes his knowledge of Islam to become the President of the *Muslim Student Association* in his university. Being a "BMOC (Big Muslim on Campus)" allows him to lead the Friday prayer, to give lectures and advice as an authentic imam, to get involved in the Palestinian cause, while being entirely self-aware of his internal distance from religion, well preserved under the camouflage of piety. After graduation the protagonist obtains a fellowship for young lawyers from the US Department of Justice and moves to Washington DC where, a few months later, he witnesses the attacks on the Pentagon and the World Trade Center on 9/11.

In the fifth part the reader finally encounters Ali Eteraz (the name means in Pakistani "Noble Protest") who loses all the comfort of his previous life – job, apartment, money, family – in the battle to "save Islam" from (some of) the Muslims. 9/11 is an awakening event to Eteraz, who now realizes that though multiple and dispersed, Islam does require submission to a heteronomous and monolingual God. The path that he imagines is reformation and, even, reinvention of Islam – through the creation of an Islamic think-tank of accomplished Muslims who would combat the monolinguism of the extremists. Yet, Eteraz is aware that Islam could not be "reformed" by the whim of some well-meaning, though alienated and widely regarded as illegitimate, American-Muslims. He travels to the Arab world to meet the *authentic* people of Islam and there he attempts to recruit Muslims who would help his cause. His rather romantic vision is to organize those Islamic reformers according to three categories that represent freedom of conscience (the new Sheikhs), freedom of expression (the Scultptors), and financial patronage (the Princesses of reformed Islam). Certainly, the attitude he actually encounters regarding his concept of Islamic reformation is far from his expectations and commitments as a reformer. However, the very fact that he has travelled the troubled journey from fundamentalism via rejection to reformation of Islam is a testimony that the original and highly sacralised covenant with Allah can take multiple directions.

Children of Dust *in the Perspective of the Western-Islamic Public Sphere*

There is, indeed, an insurmountable tension in the relationship between religion and civilization. Whatever the merits of *Children of Dust* as a literary text, its ultimate political and poetical importance is in revealing and addressing creatively some of those structural ambiguities. Despite any bona fide intention for dialogue between *Civitas Dei* and *Civitas terrena* – which in one way or another is the goal of the Western-Islamic public sphere – those ambiguities cannot be simply overlooked. The symbolic struggle between religious submission and rejection for the sake of civilization is embedded in the Quranic narrative itself; moreover, it is, actually, intrinsic to the very roots of the monotheistic scripture since its earliest forms. The parable of Habil and Qabil, who are in fact the doubles of the Old Testament's Abel and Cain, is paradigmatic in that respect and it is not difficult to see how Ali Eteraz re-appropriates this enormous monotheistic drama in his own biographical narrative. Eteraz is simultaneously the one character or the other who constantly tries to resolve this permanent ambiguity between salvation and civilization, between Habil and Qabil, between Allah and the Earthly community (the *ummah*) in all its historical forms.

The first builder of cities in the monotheistic tradition was Cain after he murdered his brother Abel and abandoned the land of God. According to the Qur'an "whoever killed a human being, except for punishment for murder or other villainy in the land, shall be deemed as though he had killed all mankind."[35] Cain (Qabil) was excluded from the salvation and community of God (the mankind that God created) and what he did after he strayed from the divine was build a city. This is an infinite symbol because Cain (Qabil) constituted the foundation of a civilization that from its very beginning was stigmatized through the fratricide. On the other hand, Abel (Habil) was the traveller and the stock breeder, the one who wandered the land without urbanizing or appropriating it, as if he himself was a living incarnation of God who is omnipresent and elusive in Islam and an anticipation of Jesus who travelled without a place "where to lay His head." Therefore, Qabil is the epitome of the horizontal transcending – the worldly corporeal domain – which has desperately severed and abandoned the link with God while Habil – the epitome of the vertical transcending – is the one murdered by the builder of cities.

Ali's covenant with Allah, in its turn, symbolizes this extremely ambiguous and intricate tension between civilization and salvation, which, it seems, could be resolved coherently only if one chooses to stick either to the horizontal or to the vertical axis. The path pointed by the Western-Islamic public sphere is – de-transcendalization and transformation of the heteronomous structures and absolutes into worldly, discursive realities: a step that does not abolish the divine but rather preserves it as a discursive structure – one among many and subject to critical examination and analysis – of the lifeworld. However, with regard to religion, as Ali Eteraz points out numerous times – and this is where the drama of the narrative resides – Islam is a mechanism for life in the extraordinary. The Islamic congregation, in that respect, with all its adjacent bifurcations, prohibitions, and rituals – or the so-called orthopraxis of Islam – does not constitute solely the skeleton of Islam. Those are significant but mostly

institutional dimensions. More importantly, the orthopraxis establishes the existential dimension of religion, namely life in the
community of salvation, which is the fundamental feature of Islam.
Islam is, first and foremost, a community of souls seeking salvation
whose main commitment is to another, non-worldly, dimension of
life, namely a commitment to the Kingdom of God.

Precisely this otherworldly dimension – this commitment to life
in the beyond – is what makes religion "religion." As Ali Eteraz
profoundly demonstrates, a covenant with Allah is impossible, or
it is an empty covenant or a semi-covenant, should this otherworldly aspect of Islam, which for the pious mind is also a
fundamental existential reality, be absent. Therefore, from Eteraz's
perspective, true reformation of religion concerns and transforms
both the vertical and the horizontal axes. If the vertical dimension
inside the Islamic origin is not rethought – with careful understanding that without the vertical dimension Islam is unthinkable –
then a true sociological crisis in the horizontal dimension is impossible to avoid. If one is confronted time and again with an
immutable vertical axis that is oblivious to the horizontal dimension and advocates blind submission to the supreme and
monological authority of the Other, then the result in the horizontal will be piety that not only dwells in the heteronomous plenitude
of God but also acts in the world solely on behalf of it. Or, in the
language of the Western-Islamic public sphere, if the relationship
between man and God is not secularized and opened to the radical interventions of history, culture, and civilization, without being
abolished, then the radical transcendence of this relationship will
continue to obliterate (as in the case of the terrorist mind) the mul-
tivalent and controversial contexts within which it exists. Religion
and the religious, if I correctly follow Ali Eteraz's project, do not
need to solve the internal tension between Habil and Qabil once
and for all; they do not need to choose one among the multiple
faces of the troubled narrator of *Children of Dust*. Rather, they
have to learn how to live simultaneously, thoroughly, and plenti-
fully with all of those faces (that are also the faces of all human
beings) and inside the internal religious aporia that has desperately
condemned humanity to both transitoriness and eternity.

The writing of Ali Eteraz is important not least because it is attentive to the stable and immutable dimension of transcendence (he
acknowledges it and attempts to be respectful of it) but also because
it shows consciousness of the political imaginary of Islam in a way

that is quite different from that of Imam Feisal Rauf. The complicated and contradictory narrative that situates Islam in various
worldly situations – in conservative Islamic schools, in the family, in
a diasporic setting, at the university, in youth and Quranic circles,
in the intimate sphere, in politics, in Pakistan as opposed to Kuwait
and the rest of the Arab world, across traditional cultures and
national boundaries – is also a way of asking what is normative in
Islam: what holds all this heterogeneity together in worldly contexts
that are so dispersed and widely varied? And, as already mentioned,
in part the answer has something to do with the theological arche of
Islam, with the radical and ahistorical transcendence internal to its
religious architecture. However, the question is crucial in a different
aspect, too. It seeks to understand how religion conditions – here
and now – subjectivities. This, in fact, is not just a theological question but also a political interrogation because it asks under what
conditions – which are always historical even if they are articulated
in most spiritual terms – certain communities of people assemble,
negotiate, and agree to worship something as divine.

The point Eteraz makes – whether intentionally or not I can
hardly say – is even more radical and complicated because he also
manages to portray Islam as a worldly force that, despite its enormous spiritual potential, has direct impact upon the creation and
transformation of social conditions, a force impacting the world
itself rather than being limited to the spiritual or the vertical domain
only. Regardless of all the theological claims that Islam might make
for atemporality and utter transcendence, its capacity to be part of
the social transformations of the world is precisely where Islam's
magnificent susceptibility to secularization resides. Despite and
beyond the fact that Islam is a congregation of the faithful, which
worships the immutable word of God embodied in the Qur'an, a
congregation that follows unquestioningly the example of the most
perfected human being, the Prophet Muhammad, and a civilization
bound by the ritual and praxis of submission to the One and only
God, Islam is also present and alive in the agency of the human
beings who are ready to argue and challenge certain or all religious
practices, to rename or negotiate them or to thoroughly refute them.
Those negotiations – as the various manifestations of the Islamic
protagonist in *Children of Dust* show – take place within the social
imaginary (they have different valences in Pakistan, in Kuwait, in
the USA, or in the wide Muslim Diaspora) and they ultimately
touch on the foundations of society with all its basic symbols and

significations, organizational principles and practices, whatever a community accepts unquestioningly and reproduces inadvertently. Therefore, the very fact that Islamic societies are different from each other, and imagine themselves differently in the multiple historical and geographical locations that they inhabit, means that society is capable of altering itself as well as the forms, conditions, and manifestations of its own being outside a strictly uniform and unilateral connection with God. The final metamorphosis in the novel, which portrays the image of the Islamic reformer – the image is taken of course as a metaphor of the human capacity to change the world here and now rather than as an enhancement of the power of worldly saviours and charismatic spiritual or political figures – somehow speaks to this radical potential of the human being to create or destroy the world and/or ultimately transform it for the world's own sake: namely, to act as a political agent.

"[T]he real covenant that guides your life, the one that you should be obsessed with, is in the service of all humanity. It's for the 'We'. It's for God. Yet you march around the world with your covenant – that false covenant – which is in the service of Muslims only, thinking yourself to be engaged in God's work. You associate partners with God. Islam is your idol."[36] In the final pages of his memoir Ali Eteraz finally manages to reconcile the concept of God with the world of human action – a proposition crucial to the Western-Islamic public sphere. If the concept of the divine is fundamental for the politico-cultural construction of the social order, it should nonetheless remain open to the various kinds of historical interventions that change or substitute this order in one way or another. The point is important because it puts the whole thinking about religion as a stable and immutable identity in the perspective of the historical movement. To be more precise, Islamic identity is no longer a stable and external framework of references but rather an open, complex, and boundless internality, which through the political agency of the human – which always happens *in* history and *as* history – is capable of unpredictable, spontaneous, and endless alterations. Inside the labyrinth of this open internality, which not only undermines the unquestionable authority of all external absolutes but also celebrates the unpredictability of human action, is where the Western-Islamic public sphere unfolds.

Poetics of Nadeem Aslam's *Maps for Lost Lovers*

"It is difficult to conceive of a more heinous, more despicable, more honourless crime. The apparent reason behind those cold-blooded, shameful murders was that the four completely innocent victims offended your completely twisted concept of honour . . . that has absolutely no place in any civilized society." Those were the words of the Ontario Superior Court Judge Robert Maranger who pronounced the verdicts against Muhammad Shafia, Tooba Yahya, and their son Hamed, found guilty of a first-degree murder in a "mass honour killing" on January 30, 2012.[37] The bodies of the three daughters of Muhammad Shafia and his first childless wife were found in June 2009 in a car submerged in a canal in Kingston. The murder, clumsily staged as an accident, was done to restore family honour when the daughters disobeyed the traditional Afghani and religious prescriptions of behaviour by "dating and acting out" while the childless wife was simply disposed of. Needless to say the Shafia case not only revived the image of 9/11 in the Canadian setting but further tarnished the most precarious and problematic aspects of the Islamic culture and tradition.

Such quotidian forms of terror, the honour killings, stay at the centre of Nadeem Aslam's novel *Maps for Lost Lovers*. Even though the action of the novel takes place in 1997 in Britain in the working class environment of Pakistani-British Muslims, and despite the fact that the novel was finished in 2004 – five years before the Shafia honour killing – it seems, quite macabrely, that the story line, semi-autobiographical and semi-fictional, meticulously portrays the Canadian tragedy from 2009. At the same time, Nadeem Aslam claims that this is a novel about 9/11, a novel in which the cosmic violence of the World Trade Center attackers blends with the mundane, elusive, and banal violence of everyday Muslim life. "In a way the book is about September 11. I asked myself whether in my personal life as a writer I had been rigorous enough to condemn the small-scale September 11s that go on every day."[38] Therefore, the best discussion of Nadeem Aslam's novel must present an awkward combination of real life references with strange temporality attached to them (9/11, the Shafia case), literary references (the fictionalized world of the main characters), Islam (which is always the main cultural and religious reference of all real life and fictional events related to the novel), and politics (regardless of the fictional element, the novel is profoundly political because it is, as its author claims, a statement on events and occurrences in the world's present day political being).

Before delving into a discussion of the political and religious aspects of *Maps for Lost Lovers* – the aspects that are closely knitted to my reflection on the Western-Islamic public sphere – I would like to make a note on the literary style of Aslam. The metaphoric, poetic, and profoundly sensuous language of the novel is more than just ornament. The poetic language has a performative function inasmuch as it truly

> counterpoints the misery imposed upon the characters. One of them says that the system, which here happens to be Islam, is based on contempt of the human body. So, I wanted to touch everyone's skin, again and again. . . . There is nothing disgusting about the physical world. I wanted to show what a brilliant phenomenon it is to actually exist within the world. And how beautiful our planet is. And yet we are surrounded by those systems that won't let us enjoy it, which is why everybody's so miserable in the novel.[39]

In that respect, the whole writing style of Nadeem Aslam is poetic and transformative in the overall political sense that I try to endorse and develop here, namely, as an art of shaping, creating, inventing, producing (always in progress) new secular forms of connection that stand outside any rigorous systems or absolutes.

I would like to emphasize also how important and political the concept of artistic creation and imagination, which always results in the shaping of new forms, is for the Western-Islamic public sphere. The root reference to creativity, which comes from the Greek *demiurgia* and later from its Latin derivation *creatio*, contains in itself an instrumentalist reference. As Stathis Gourgouris makes evident, the notion derives its meaning from the public sphere as a combination of the words *demos* (people) and *ergon* (work).[40] In Plato, there is a distinction between the *demiourgos* as simply a worker and the poet as the one who creates and invents forms.[41] Later on, because of the Christian modification of the term, *demiourgos* is related to creation out of the Absolute. For Plato, however, the invention of forms is always somehow connected to an undesirable deformation and alteration. The reason he exiles the poet from the polis is precisely because the poet, as an inventor of forms, has the power to transform ethics or public morals, an act which is political in essence. Therefore, Plato's apprehension about the power of the poetical contains something that later on will become a major philosophical and theological concern, namely the fear of alteration and the desire for an anchored, unalterable, and inalienable truth. Certainly, this is because the power of poetic transformation does not only engage in the production of otherness as an internal, in purely materialistic terms, process, and thus questions otherness as an external phenomenon, but also because the poetic contains an aspect of destruction. There is no external guarantee, no God or other Absolute, that can save or prevent the moment of alteration from being potentially a moment of destruction.

Interestingly enough, this primal Platonian fear of the creative, transformative, and possibly destructive power of poetic language has durable effects in the formation of modernity, in the aspect of modernity's obsession with scientific knowledge, foundational truths, and instrumental technical, monetary, and militaristic logic. In that aspect, too, modernity shares a number of structural similarities with the rigid theological imaginary, from which the model of the Western-Islamic public sphere attempts to depart. The Platonian anxiety is also encoded in the classical distinction between private and public, where the role of the poet (and the writer and the intellectual) as an inventor of new forms and horizons is undermined and replaced by the role of the expert whose knowledge is always measurable and allegedly rational. What is remarkable about Nadeem Aslam's poetics (and generally about the intellectual work that the Western-Islamic public sphere recognizes and celebrates, in a sense), therefore, is the ability – even at the level of language in Aslam's case or at the level of abstract thought in the case of other Muslim intellectuals – to engage the frauds and variations of strict religious theology as the original and indisputable centre of knowledge and history. The thick, sensuous, dense, and highly metaphorical language of Nadeem Aslam, which captures the world in microscopic detail – "glint-slippered frosts," blown rose heads lying in clusters like "bright droppings of fantastic creatures," "the white fur necktie of a moth," "naan bread shaped like ballet slippers, poppy seeds that were coarser than sand grains," "chilli seeds that were volts of electricity, the peppers whose stalks were hooked like umbrella handles," "small antlers of smoke rising from incense sticks," Muslim angels dressed in silk and brocade with multicolored wings, dead tulips lean out of "a bin like the necks of a drunk swan," etc. – does produce the world of Islam anew as something material, corporeal, and alive, something that could be touched and penetrated, as something profoundly genuine and deeply ingrained in the physical reality. There is a reference in one of the scenes to Islamic folklore saying that the peacock inadvertently let Satan into the garden of Eden; the two missing characters in the novel, at a certain point, are imagined as transformed into peacocks.[42] In another interview Nadeem Aslam shares, "I wanted every chapter of *Maps for Lost Lovers* to be like a Persian miniature. In these miniatures a small piece of paper – no bigger than a sheet of A4 – holds an immense wealth of beauty, colour and detail. Trees have leaves each perfectly rendered. Flowers are moments old and the tilework of the palaces and mosques is lovingly detailed. That was the aim in *Maps*."[43]

All the literary references that inhabit the prose of Aslam – from *One Thousand and One Nights*, from the literary and poetic tradition of the Indian subcontinent, as well as from the Qur'an and the hadiths – restage the Islamic tradition as a radical present exceeding any traditional narration or symbolization of Islam. Literally the world of Islam in *Maps for Lost Lovers* happens, changes, transforms itself out of language's multiple and basically infinite grammatical forms. Precisely this capacity of the poetic to change and transform, which I do not grasp as a mere abstraction but as an active and live performance, is where its political force resides. Since its ancient signification, this energy of the poetical belongs to humanity's capacity to both imagine the world and also to encounter it in all its immanent dimensions. This is precisely the reason why, as one of the protagonists intelligently observes, "language could provide some refuge from terror."[44]

Plot and Themes

[They] seemed to know how to blend together all that life contains, the real truth, the undeniable last word, the innermost core of all that is unbearably painful within a heart and all that is joyful, all that is loved and all that is worthy of love but remains unloved, lied to and lied about, the unimaginable depths of the soul where no other can withstand the longing and which few have the conviction to plumb, the sorrows and the indisputable rage.[45]

This observation, made about jazz music in the beginning of *Maps for Lost Lovers*, acts as an anticipatory and abstract summary of the main themes of the novel. Behind this rich atmospheric description lurk, in an intricate intertwinement, the anonymous British town, renamed by its South-Asian inhabitants as Dasht-e-Tanhaii (Urdu. The Desert of Loneliness); the unresolved murder of Chanda and Jugnu, the two unmarried lovers who lived together out of wedlock; and the convoluted life narratives of Shamas (Jugnu's brother), who in his mid-sixties is a former Pakistani poet and a current British social worker married to an exceedingly religious wife, Kaukab. Their three children, Ujala, Charag, and Mah-Jabin, have already left home at the start of the novel to escape the world of religious oppression and restriction inflicted on them by their mother. Religion, as one of the characters of the novel observes, is often another source of torture for millions of suffering people. Fear of Allah's punishment also infects the life of Suraya, a divorced woman, who tempts Shamas into a hurried marriage and then hurried divorce in order to be able, following the Islamic law, to remarry her previous husband in Pakistan, who had divorced her carelessly pronouncing the Arab word *talaq* (I divorce you) three times in a drunken moment.

All of the characters that Aslam depicts are complex and unfinished and any attempt at a presentation is doubtlessly limited and doomed to bias from the outset. However, there is a certain purposefully accomplished contrast in the build-up of the main characters. Shamas is portrayed as a liberal and secular person, well-integrated into the British milieu, while his wife is a pious, uncompromising, and somewhat blinkered follower of Islam for whom "too much freedom isn't good for anyone or anything."[46] Their personal relationship, as well as the lenses through which they perceive and connect to the outside world, are coloured simultaneously by fascinations and negotiations with fundamentalism and racism, religion, and secular modernity. Yet those awkward perceptions and connections all describe at once a claustrophobic world of loneliness and isolation and present the reader with a meditation on global affairs after 9/11.

The Pakistani-dominated neighbourhood Aslam depicts is a "place of Byzantine intrigue and emotional espionage, where when two people stop to talk on the street their tongues are like the two halves of a scissor coming together, cutting reputations and good names to shreds."[47] Doubtlessly full of small, corporeal, and sensuous wonders, the world of *Maps for Lost Lovers* is also full of cruelty committed in the name of holy terrors. They arise not partly from the fact that two brothers from the neighbourhood kill their sister and her lover for living in sin and ruining the family reputation. After all, from the perspective of the killers, Chanda and Jugnu are guilty of a sin and subject to punishments that "are of divine origin and cannot be judged by human criteria."[48] Aslam also suggests that these actions stem from a culture of oppression directly related to the religious habitat of Islam and not restricted by or adherent to the prescriptions of the Qur'an only. The charge that Aslam makes is not so much against the sacred text of Islam inasmuch as it is clear that the Qur'an itself does not prescribe or excuse honour killings.[49] Yet Islam is guilty of something Nadeem Aslam describes as a particular religious habitual culture, which, deeply anchored in religious certainty, allows mothers to abort female fetuses, exorcists or respected imams to beat unruly girls to death, honoured clerics to rape young boys, vicious gossip to ruin defiant women, failure to demoralize frustrated men, and drunken husbands to rape or divorce by whim their wives, a culture that allows humans, in general, to be reduced to a state of moral idiocy that excuses or ignores any abuse only to protect Islam from outside critique. This state of moral helplessness is certainly transparent behind one of the most often repeated phrases in the novel: Allah's law is Allah's law and cannot be questioned. Aslam himself, who was raised in poor immigrant Muslim towns in the North of England, maintains in an interview that family life in numerous Western Muslim ghettos is "frequently reduced to nothing more than legalized brutality."[50] To ignore the fact that this culture of oppression is related to the religious and legal universe of Islam as an everyday lived practice means more or less to avoid addressing the problem of culturally and communally driven violence at its core.

And indeed, this last statement (Nadeem Aslam's) could be easily confirmed not only by the recent honour killing of the four Shafia women that scandalized Canada but also by data presented in government and media reports on honour killings. In 2011, for example, nearly 3000 cases of honour attacks were reported in the UK, 1000 women were murdered in Pakistan for allegedly defaming family honour, 720 died in family disputes in Sindh, and 300 cases of honour killings were reported in Turkey.[51] "A woman in one Pakistani province is killed every 38 hours," claims Aslam, who is eager to remind that each shocking crime in his novel is based on a true case.[52] A woman is murdered and her killer is partly exonerated on the grounds of honour or cultural specificity. Does this mean, however, that the culture label should protect and safeguard any interrogation, first, into the legitimacy of those crimes and, second, into the sacred roots that sanction them? Aslam certainly dramatizes the answer to that question:

> They boasted of having killed her and Jugnu – but only in Pakistan, where the laws and the religion and the customs reinforced their sense of having acted properly, legitimately, correctly. The people who learned of their crime patted their backs and said they had fulfilled their obligation, that such sons were born only to men among men and women among women.[53]

After the announcement of the verdict in an English court, however, the only refuge for the two brothers and murderers of Chanda and Jugnu is to shout litanies of the racism and prejudice inflicted on them as a minority by a country of "prostitutes and homosexuals" who have insulted the culture and religion of Islam. Muhammad Shafia, the father of the three girls killed in Kingston, told his second wife and son the night before he was arrested for the murder: "I am happy and my conscience is clear. They haven't done good and God punished them."[54] Later on, the police revealed tapes on which Muhammad Shafia overtly admitted the crimes as committed, among other things, in the name of God: "They committed treason from beginning to end. They betrayed kindness, they betrayed Islam, they betrayed our religion and creed, they betrayed our tradition. . . . God curse their graduation! Curse of God on both of them, on their kind. God's curse on them for a generation! May the devil shit on their graves! Is that what a daughter should be? Would she be such a whore?"[55]

One possible accusation against Nadeem Aslam is that in *Maps for Lost Lovers* he portrays the worst aspects of Islam and thus nourishes the fantasies of the already numerous Islamophobes in the West. Despite the fact that Aslam approaches the intricate world of Islam with meticulous understanding, care, and affection, he is doubtlessly sensitive to the extremes of the arguments that usually govern all the debates that concern the presence, visibility, and demands of Islam in Western settings. The seemingly clear-cut East-West divide is purposefully encoded in the portrayal of Shamas and Kaukab yet the distinction is also a consciously sought sociological perspective. A Pakistani character in the novel is angry with the West: "The West is full of hypocrites who kill our people with impunity and say it's all a matter of principle and justice but when we do the same thing they say our definition of "principle" and "justice" is flawed."[56] Elsewhere, Kaukab voices a complex of the Pakistani minority in England: "the white police are interested in us Pakistanis only when there is a chance to prove that we are savages who slaughter our sons and daughters, brothers and sisters."[57] The other perspective, of the majority that encounters the Islamic other is also tentatively described:

> The parents of a seven-year old Muslim child . . . had been summoned to the headmistress's office yesterday and informed that the boy had been telling his white schoolmates that they were all going to be skinned alive in Hell for eating pork and that their mummies and daddies would be set on fire and made to drink hot water because they drank alcohol and did not believe in Allah and Muhammad, peace be upon him.[58]

On the other hand, those Muslims who have managed to abandon the world of violence of the poor Muslim ghettos and to receive Western educations often encounter the distrust and prejudice of the dominant culture. A British man in the novel calls an upper-class, Cambridge-educated Pakistani woman "a darkie bitch" and her only reaction is to blame this attitude on the poor neighbour-hood of her origin, full of Pakistanis she qualifies as "sister-murdering, nose-blowing, mosque-going, cousin-marrying, veil-wearing inbred imbeciles."[59] And again Aslam intertwines in that moment the echo of Kaukab, who recognizes in the well-educated Pakistani woman a traitor: "We are driven out of our countries because of people like her, the rich and the powerful. We leave because we never have any food or dignity because of their selfish behavior. And now they resent our being here too. Where are we supposed to go?"[60]

Maps for Lost Lovers *in the Perspective of the Western-Islamic Public Sphere*

It is an indisputable fact that Nadeem Aslam is a talented writer, Muslim, and Western intellectual simultaneously, who describes artfully and movingly the troubled habitat of Western Islam. It is also evident that in his prose Aslam is at once a social historian and a poet, a realist narrator and a romantic dreamer. There is, however, another, political quality to his writing, namely the internal conviction that literary language and exposition could affect and transform the social world, and this exceeds all previous characteristics, putting Aslam's prose on par with the hermeneutic efforts in Islamic theology of such figures as Muhammad Arkoun, Nasr Abu Zayd, and Abdelkarim Soroush, among others. Nadeem Aslam's commitments and writing, interestingly enough, are also similar to the reflections of Pascal Bruckner on guilt in chapter 3.

In this section I would like to return again to the complex topic of guilt, which ended the third chapter in order to elaborate further on the central thesis of the book: the Western-Islamic public sphere, as a secular practice of critique, experimentation, and interrogation, is possible only outside the confines of the rigorous, immutable, and unquestionable theological imaginary, which also means outside the confines of guilt. I am completely aware that Nadeem Aslam does not attack the formal theology of Islam but the lived practices of religion codified in the ways people experience and relate to the world that surrounds them (but, after all, what is the point of theology if it is not dressed in the praxis of religion?). However, even if one is tempted by a precarious conclusion, it is difficult not to notice the alliance between, on the one hand, exceedingly and dangerously violent practices of oppression on a mass scale in the poverty-stricken neighbourhoods of Islam in Western societies and, on the other hand, an immutable corpora of sacred prescriptions, always adamantly preserved from encroachment by various pious authorities, which in their otherworldly perfection are readily prepared to say what and who is destined for hell or paradise. I have also no doubt that the nefarious chemistry of this alliance, reinforced by practices of prejudice, imperial politics, and military interventions that have frequently defined the terms of Western politics vis-à-vis Islam since the period of colonialism, is responsible today for the ghettoization and segregation of the Muslim communities in the West. The fact that those sacred texts, the people who live by their letter (or for that matter against it), and the cold military and instrumental logic of the Western colonizer are all in time and, regardless of all the absolutisms and certainties that determine them, they all have to experience time's movement; its unpredictable and unknowable direction and insecurity are what I use consistently as argument for the immanent, inevitable, and unfinished secularization of the world. The Western-Islamic public sphere is an intellectual universe deeply rooted in critique, interrogation, and doubt, which are inherent in the process of secularization inasmuch as the latter, as a process, is not obedient to predetermined structures of God or Reason and it does not exist outside a specific worldly encounter.

Pascal Bruckner, in his recent book *Tyranny of Guilt* (as already mentioned in chapter 3), identifies fascism, communism, genocide, slavery, racism, and imperialism as major historical reasons for Western guilt vis-à-vis the impoverished and underdeveloped parts of the rest of world.[61] Yet, guilt, according to Bruckner, has turned into a Western pathology, today, that obscures such important realities as the fact that, first, the West does not hold a monopoly on evil – it exists across societies and cultures – and, second, the West has created but also destroyed monsters, abolished slavery, renounced colonialism, built communal solidarities, and struggled to establish rules and institutions in respect of human dignity. Guilt, Bruckner argues, prevents Western democracies from naming, let alone fighting, today's atrocities, which come along with contemporary forms of racism, religious fundamentalism, and cultural conservation. Radical Islam – in the forms meticulously depicted by Nadeem Aslam – Bruckner does not hesitate to define as an executioner of Western democracy and not as its victim. The larger point that Pascal Bruckner makes, however, is that this kind of Western obsession with guilt and remorse makes a critical perspective towards non-Western forms of violence impossible (even if they exist inside the Western setting) and it condemns both Western and non-Western cultures to the impotence of identity politics. Guilt, moreover, constitutes a fundamental theological moment, and, in its function, it strikingly approximates the cultures based on unquestionable and eternal foundations, regardless of whether or not the latter are inspired by the seemingly different terrains of God or Reason.

Guilt is the religious modus vivendi in *Maps for Lost Lovers*. It always returns to the crime scene, as something final and irreducible, in order to remind that the plenitude of sin and time are shattered to pieces by the superior and timeless divine knowledge of what is right and wrong once and forever in human relations. Guilt, however, Nadeem Aslam suggests, is a divine sickness because it erases all the happy coincidences of time and the world and prevents any sense of personhood and agency, which could be achieved only if one is aware of their mortality inside an anonymous and undying universe. For the guilt-ridden mortality there is no chance to get in touch with the world, to encounter its movement and constant change, to imagine the world and experience its melancholy, but rather it is a deserved punishment. After all, in the grand eschatological picture of the universe, drawn by various prophets, what matters is the promise of immortality after one gets punished for one's actual worldly, and presumably fallen, encounters. Guilt, moreover, deprives people of their fundamental right to question the law, to rebel against it as citizens, and, if only for that reason, it is a fundamentally non-political principle. Those citizens who abide by the prescriptions of the One and the Only God (or law) and live with the fear of guilt annihilate their own political being, choosing to be comfortably sheltered in the humble confines of Piety. For that reason guilt is excluded from the praxis of the Western-Islamic public sphere because it is incommensurable with the demands of political life inasmuch as political life means free life, a life that dares to stand against all kinds of ideologies.

Orhan Pamuk's *My Name is Red*

Pope Benedict XVI's lecture at Regensburg delivered on September 12, 2006, entitled "Faith, Reason and the University – Memories and Reflections," stirred a certain controversy in the world of Islam. The line that provoked a great deal of discussion was this: "Show me just what Muhammad brought that was new, and there you will find things that are only wicked and inhuman, such as his command to spread by the sword the faith he preached."[62] Despite the fact that this lecture was not directed towards Islam but rather addressed contemporary practices of Christianity (and a careful analysis conveys that in it the Pope celebrated Christian dogma and heteronomy in an intriguing and no less powerful way than a respected Muslim theologian would do with respect to the Islamic dogma), the anti-Islamic sentiment inherent in it rephrased in theological language some central Western concerns about Islam: a religion primarily predicated on the absolute will of Allah, without presenting a supporting social theology that narrates how this divine will crafts a reasonable, ordered universe, renders dialogue impossible and provides reasons for violent conflict.

The fact that in Islam there is a long rationalist tradition that revolves around the medieval theological and intellectual school of the Mut'azilites and inspires much of the Quranic hermeneutics initiated today by other contemporary Muslim intellectuals is something I have already discussed in chapters 2 and 3 of the book. Here, my intention is to open another door of possible engagement via the Western-Islamic public sphere, one which does not rely as much on the various manifestations of reason in a comparative perspective as on the investigation of beauty and art as a new meaningful avenue of connection. The tradition of beauty also has a long history in Islam, broadly known as the '*ihsaani* tradition' (meaning literally in Arabic "to be beautiful or good"). As Joseph Lumbard, a scholar of classical Islam, suggests, the Qur'an itself defines God as the first creator of beauty. [63] Probably this is the reason why in one hadith, considered truthful in the Sunni tradition of Islam, Muhammad exclaims: "Oh, God, you have made beautiful my creation (Arab. *khalq*), make beautiful my character (Arab. *khuluq*)."[64] The historical involvement of this tradition in shaping the cultural and religious universe of Islam as well as its establishment as simultaneously a site of conflict and connection with the West is certainly a central topic in the overall oeuvre of one of the most distinguished contemporary novelists of Muslim origin, Orhan Pamuk.

The 2006 Nobel Prize for Literature established Orhan Pamuk firmly as a master writer (the second youngest intellectual to receive the Novel Prize in its history) and also as one of the literary figures of the twentieth century who, in the words of the Swedish Academy, "has discovered new symbols for the clash and interlacing of cultures."[65] Orhan Pamuk, unlike the other intellectuals discussed in the book, has spent most of his life in his home country, Turkey. He belongs to critical Islam, however, not only because his work, which is dedicated to topics dealing with the encounter between the worlds of Islam and the West, conceives of a shared yet tortured universe beyond violence, dogma, and submission, but also because of his persistent presence, for more than thirty years, in the international literary scene as a recipient of numerous prestigious literary awards in France, Italy, England, Ireland, and USA, among other countries. Pamuk is also an honorary member of the American Academy of Arts, a yearly visiting scholar and lecturer at Columbia University,[66] and truly a cosmopolitan intellectual whose artistic engagements with Islam, which may be labeled in different ways,[67] could not be ignored. He himself admits:

> I learn and pick-up from other authors. I've learned from Thomas Mann . . ., Italo Calvino . . ., Umberto Eco, Marguerite Yourcenar.

. . . What inspired me most for *My Name is Red* were the Islamic miniatures . . . drawn to illustrate the best scenes of stories that once upon a time everyone knew by heart and today, because of westernization, very few remember.[68]

Insofar as my argument about critical Islam presupposes literature's unique relationship to knowledge and critique, the engagement with Pamuk's novel *My Name Is Red* offered here is essentially political: it is based on the understanding that the literary always pertains to the domains of the social, the historical, and the worldly and thus, by the virtue of its mere existence, it disputes the ahistorical claims of any heteronomy. Moreover, the interrogation of the poetical elements of a text also attempts understanding what determines the parameters of social poesis itself. Precisely for this reason, the analysis through the lenses of the Western-Islamic public sphere goes beyond the disciplinary confines of aesthetic theory or literary criticism and it is a political or culturological analysis in essence: it seeks to describe and determine the main performative moments in the social imagination involved in the Western-Islamic encounter. In that respect it is not mere coincidence that Orhan Pamuk – an intellectual and literary figure – was tried in 2005 for "insulting Turkishness" for remarks he made in front of a Swedish newspaper about the deaths of 30 000 people in the ongoing Turkish-Kurdish military conflict in the South-East of the country and also about the Armenian genocide that took place on the Turkish territory during the first world war. "Nobody but me dares to talk about it," Pamuk simply declared as if to confirm that an engagement with the historical and the political is always deeply ingrained in the craft and conscience of the literary master and public intellectual.[69] Probably this is the reason why, during the trial, rallies were triggered to burn Pamuk's books.

Plot and Structure

My Name Is Red is set in Istanbul in 1591, in the period when the Ottoman Empire begins to experience a gradual decline in its institutional and power structures. The drama of this decline is narrated in the timeframe of the nine-day period following the murder of Elegant, one of the master miniaturists in the Ottoman court. Elegant and three other miniaturists (Stork, Butterfly, and Olive) are secretly commissioned by Enishte, a servant of the Ottoman sultan and a former ambassador to Venice and moderately talented illustrator himself, to create an illustrated and illuminated book in the style of the Western perspective painting to be sent to the Venetian Doge. The paintings imitating the European Renaissance manner aim to affirm the Ottoman supremacy over the East and the West, to depict the sultan's ultimate domination in the artistic language of the West, and, mostly, to capture the dramatic encounter between two distinct ways of seeing the world: the Islamic and the Western.

The Islamic way of seeing in *My Name Is Red* is neatly related to miniature painting where images are not treated as independent artistic realities but rather as part of the craft of the book; they are 'footnotes' to the text or its extensions and for that reason their masters are always anonymous. Here is how one of the miniaturists in the novel, Olive, explains the relationship between image and word: "Allah created this worldly realm so that, above all, it might be seen. Afterward, He provided us with words so that we might share and discuss with one another what we've seen. We mistakenly assumed that these stories arose out of words and that illustrations were painted in the service of these stories."[70] Therefore, seeing is what precedes the word in the aesthetic system of Islam, which allows painting of images and generally visual representation to thrive only as discreet stylizations that accompany literature.[71] Therefore, classical Islamic images do not represent real life but only externalize the internal life of the narrative. Painting, therefore, within the iconoclastic Islamic tradition, is a controversial topic inasmuch as it concentrates in itself the classical Western notions of style, artistic self-expression, and representation. In the sixteenth century, Western painting, first in Italy and then in other parts of Europe, had already achieved its autonomy from narrativity, and the story of the image itself had become the object of art independent of religious, mythical, or epic texts.[72] Therefore, from a strictly religious standpoint, the three-dimensional images of the European Renaissance (which include human perspective) are regarded as an arrogant claim on the part of the painter to be as creative and imaginative as Allah himself, which certainly constitutes a mortal sin for the pious followers of Islam. Renaissance painting prioritizes a human perspective over the divine and thus neglects the Islamic search for a divine vision reflected in the miniatures, namely "the act of seeking out Allah's memories and seeing the world as He sees the world."[73] The miniatures in the secret book also contain a portrait of the Ottoman sultan, who has obviously fallen victim to the temptation of having his face naturalistically depicted and not drawn as any face in a miniature, which should duplicate an Eastern Asian template.

Enishte (meaning uncle in Turkish) summons for the task of painting the secret book his nephew Kara (meaning black in Turkish), who has been in exile for twelve years. Kara (or Black), as the reader learns, was forced to leave Istanbul because of his avowed passion for his uncle's daughter, Shekure, which he revealed at the time via the art of the portraiture. He announced his love by repainting a scene from *Khusrev and Shirin* – a popular Persian love story and a popular subject among the miniaturists – following Bihzad, one of the most prominent Persian masters. In the classical twelfth-century Persian tale, Shirin, who is an Armenian princess, falls in love with Khusrev, the prince of Persia, upon seeing his picture. While repainting the story, Black substitutes the nondescript faces of Shirin and Khusrev with his own face and with Shekure's, led by the conviction that the anonymity of the classical Muslim genre of drawing cannot sufficiently communicate love. Banned from the family and Istanbul for his audacity, Black ironically comes back to participate with his skills in the preparation of the secret book of the sultan. Also, in order to marry Shekure, he has to solve the chain of murders that began with his arrival. All the discussions on art, life, and religion about both the Eastern and the Western traditions, therefore, are intricately enmeshed in a narrative that has a touch of both detective story and romance.

As the story unfolds, Black has access to a wide collection of masterpieces kept in the sultan's treasury as well as to the master miniaturist of the sultan, Master Osman. They spend together two nights at the Imperial Treasury studying the miniatures in the secret book trying to determine the style of the paintings found on Elegant's corpse and thus identify the murderer. Master Osman recognizes Olive's style but also blinds himself on the spot with Bihzad's needle in order to protect his own vision from Western influences by reaching the state of ultimate darkness, or "God's pureness." He notes, while with Black, that the old masters "would suffer pangs of conscience about changing their talent, colors and methods. They'd consider it dishonorable to see the world one day as an Eastern shah commanded, the next, as a Western ruler did – which is what the artists of our day do." [74] Olive, on the other hand, is a truly tragic character. His obsession with Western painting leads him not only to the murders of Elegant and Uncle (the one for being overtly pious and traditional and the other for being excessively Westernized and modern), to a hubristic desire to paint his self-portrait in the space of the miniature designated for the sultan's portrait, and also to the tragic realization that, despite talent, the European tradition of painting requires knowledge and proficiency that he and the other miniaturists do not possess; the whole concept of a productive encounter between the two styles of painting and seeing – the Western and the Islamic – is nothing, a pure imitation without artistic quality, if it is not invested with mastery and knowledge. Westernization, Olive discovers, could be a dangerous road because, instead of originality, it could inflict mere imitation. When finally Black blinds Olive with Bihzad's needle (failing to kill him), Olive expresses a tragically reflected bias against the sultan's project: "For the rest of your lives you'll do nothing but emulate the Franks for the sake of an individual style. . . . But precisely because you emulate the Franks, you'll never attain individual style."[75]

Politics of the Literary Masterpiece

My Name Is Red is an extraordinary literary work – a masterpiece.[76] Not only because it has a complex narrative model where it tells the story of a series of murders, set in the sixteenth-century Ottoman world that revolves around an unfinished masterpiece but also because of the structural characteristics of the text itself. On the literary plane, Pamuk successfully enmeshes the elements of the Ottoman historiography and Turkish story telling (widely inspired by the Arab-Islamic tradition of *One Thousand and One Nights,* but the novel also weaves stories from across all of the Islamic world: Turkmen, Mongol, Indian, Chinese, and Persian) with techniques of heteroglossic Western writing. On the aesthetic plane, the text explores the intricacies and awkward encounters between the Eastern and the Western visual cultures. Also, being a political allegory, the novel dramatizes the weakening and eventual decline of the Ottoman empire, torn between the pious traditionalism of Islam and the Renaissance impulses, coming from the West, that shake to the core the aesthetic, political, and everyday worlds of the empire. Islam in the book is another extremely complex layer; on the one hand, many of the characters interweave Quranic interpretations in their everyday monologues and thus present a version of Islam that is mundane, alive, and true to the lifeworld experiences depicted in the novel. On the other hand, a memorable quote from the Qur'an, a phrase that belongs to Satan in surah 2:26 – *To God belongs the East and the West* – somehow frames the other layers suggesting that the separation of the world into two poles is Satan's work. And finally is the layer that is the most subtle and related to the poetic substance of the novel: while the Qur'an is the divine masterpiece and the ultimate reference framework to all discussions of art and aesthetics, the novel itself, through its very structure, multiplicity, language, and experimental engagement with the questions of life, beauty, and death, puts the divine into a perspective and thus questions the universal pretensions of the sacred. The Qur'an is a divine masterpiece while the novel is a human masterpiece and they both compete, in different ways, to invent the main tropes of the social-historical imagination. After all, the masterpiece (as any master narrative) turns out to be a human invention despite the fact that the sacralized language in which it is depicted belongs to the registers of the transcendental, immutable, and eternal.

My Name Is Red is a literary masterpiece not only because it explores a range of extremely complex themes, which, hidden behind the anachronistic sixteenth century, actually pertain to modern day dilemmas (mainly around the East-West dichotomy), but also because of its structural polyphonic design. The novel's polyphony – the story is recounted in 21 distinct voices including those of the corpses, the color red, Satan, a dog, a gold coin, the elements in the miniatures, etc. – challenges the monological structure of the sacred text by relativizing any dogmatism and, indeed, by reducing much of the religious message to one discourse among others. Dealing with a similar literary context, Sadia Abbas asks if a religious novel could be written at all, by which she means a novel that does not void the voice of God.[77] This is an important question and, as far as my analysis goes, Orhan Pamuk attempts a referentially serious discussion of religion in *My Name Is Red* without, however, abandoning his critical intellectual task of asking how the social imaginary that posits God and all the divine paraphernalia as a foundational social institution might alter if challenged by human imagination. Pamuk initiates this discussion via the medium of the novel and more specifically through what is intrinsically literary and also political about it (at least to my mind): namely, the production of knowledge (of which critique is an essential).

Therefore, the competition between novelistic writing and the Qur'an that is magnificently staged in *My Name Is Red* has a theoretical dimension beyond the basic plot line and its multifarious ramifications. The murder that frames the novel facilitates, ironically, a new way of seeing by rupturing the text and opening possibilities for the voicing of different perspectives and the participation of different narrators. This multiplicity of points of view is the most crucial challenge to submissive religion. It is also basically a poetic articulation of the human-centered, worldly, social imagination that begins to be celebrated historically with the Renaissance and whose final institutionalization comes with the establishment of the category of "literature" by European Romanticism, understood here as an extension of the Enlightenment project. Yet Pamuk's writing is different from the worldliness of the Romantic idealism (whose social project aims to re-signify the role and function of the poet in the world), which, even in its most crucial moments of radical thinking, constitutes itself around such heteronomous categories as the sublime, the genius, the spirit, the absolute, etc. All of these categories, which appear to be central to all aesthetic discussions that permeate the novel, are in the final account destabilized. What seems to concern Orhan Pamuk is not, strictly speaking, the intrinsic value of the different aesthetic projects of the Eastern and Western traditions; the categories of good, beautiful, truthful, or sublime, even though significant, are not what makes an aesthetic object, including a literary text, a point of connection but rather what enables those objects to frame a domain of cognition or, in other words, a perspective from which one can think and produce knowledge. For example, the murderer's hand is described in the novel as an object of sublime aesthetics, a hand which simultaneously draws and kills: "I could see no one color and realized that all colors had become red. What I thought was my blood was red ink; what I thought was ink on his hands was my flowing blood."[78] And yet, what remains central to the novel is not the murder itself but the literary performative gesture, always in a specific point in time, that stages the murder as one of the horizons that makes the conversation on style possible.

Pamuk's sensitivity towards the performative value of aesthetic objects and literary writing further conveys his delicate engagement with the divine. It has to be said that literature, unlike religion, does not have an a priori cognitive object. Instead, each text or aesthetic experience possess its own object of knowledge, which may be different each time depending on their forms, horizons, or possibilities, as well as on the conditions under which they are read or experienced. By contrast, it is impossible for God to be a performer, Pamuk reminds the reader repeatedly by bringing the conversation back to the eternal perspective of Allah, because God's domain, theologically speaking, cannot be reduced to the contingent nature of the performative act. What, therefore, makes *My Name Is Red* a different kind of masterpiece from the sacred text is the novel's awareness of the capacity of the literary to alter the conditions of action and perception within a changing socio-historical landscape. This performativeness also makes the literary or aesthetic object of knowledge a matter of praxis, i.e. it is always involved in a process of movement and transformation. In an insightful passage, which is actually a conversation between the murderer and Enishte, Pamuk admits what the novel (and not only a miniature painting) aims to accomplish:

> What your pen draws is neither truthful nor frivolous! When you portray a crowd gathering, the tension emerging from the glances between figures, their position on the page and the meaning of the text metamorphose into an elegant eternal whisper. I return to your paintings again and again to hear that whisper, and each time, I realize with a smile that the meaning has changed, and how shall I put it, I begin to read the painting anew. When the layers of meaning are taken together, a depth emerges that surpasses even the perspectivism of the European masters.[79]

All of these intrinsic literary qualities of the novel actually speak to *My Name Is Red*'s political significance. According to my argument, the political thrives in an atmosphere – in this case a literary atmosphere – which is neither rationalist-scientific nor apocalyptic (dogmatic-religious). Rather, the political is fully possible in a universe where thought is a poetic force. I am drawing here partly on an argument developed theoretically in Davide Panagia's *The Poetics of Political Thinking* where he posits the poetics of political thinking as a condition for pluralism "that looks to the interactive intensity of difference in itself as a source for novel forms of political association."[80] What I understand by poetic thought is related to society's power to imagine and re-create itself radically by inventing itself as an other (as somebody else); this is another way to say that the poetical capacity of humanity for the re-invention of itself as something/someone different is related to the issues of pluralism and democracy. This makes the literary text linked to the social-imaginary domain, or basically this is a claim insisting that the literary domain, or more precisely the literary fantasy, is a political matter. Orhan Pamuk's writing is fully aware of this. How?

Pamuk's prose is written as an argument suggesting that funda-mentalism (religious or secularist, of the past or of the present) is not an issue of nature (there is no heteronomous reality that exists just by itself precisely because its authorization will have to be external to social and political life) but of history. It appears at a certain socio-historical juncture. The real task of the intellectual writer then is to expose the process of blind subjection by revealing the historicity of any absolutist thinking, which means also to account simultaneously for this thinking's historical peculiarity and trans-historical perpetuity. To understand religious heteronomy then, especially as it is lived historically and presently in the Turkish cultural context but also beyond it, a specific historical-cultural trajectory has to be followed (the Ottoman context, the encounter with the Renaissance, the symbolic and literal overcoming of the religious tradition, the individual drama, the secularist state, the rebellion against it, Western and Eastern art, political changes, etc.). Moreover, Pamuk very shrewdly suggests that no society, even the most conservative and absolutist one (as the fifteenth- and the sixteenth-century Ottoman society is), is constituted around a once-and-for-all, final, self-fulfilled imaginary. There are always 'cracks' that question and challenge the tradition, religion, God (as the dominant tropes of the social world), and in *My Name Is Red* those cracks come in the form of foreign images (or discussions on art). Yet, tradition, religion, and God always work to perpetuate them-selves and sometimes this happens through the incorporation of foreign elements. Pamuk is interested, therefore, in the ongoing process of encounter between the East and the West (two very much reified identity principles), which may be circuitous and retrogres-sive but in all instances is unpredictable. At the same time, those living and interacting antagonisms that define the novel but also define much of what is signified in reality by East and West also, in a more abstract sense, pertain to the workings of culture in the making of history where the literary is an essential part.

Unlike sacred scripture, literary writing, Pamuk's project reminds us, has the capacity to extend its work to those historical elements that testify to humanity's radical ability for poetic re-inven-tion because it is interested, as *My Name Is Red* suggests, in what challenges and subverts cultural norms. In that respect, the whole novel, not just as a literary piece but as a complex work of culture, is a performative terrain where the encounter between the East (via the Qur'an and the miniature painting) and the West (via the human-centered perspective of the world) ritualizes its hopes and fears, its values and beliefs, and its fantasies about what is the East and what is the West and who is the other. And at the same time, the novel stages other images of the same binary, other self-repre-sentations that may, under different historical conditions (those of the present day, for example), lead to (self-)critique or interroga-tion of those binaries and indeed to their (self-)alteration. This is the performative force of the literary, which Orhan Pamuk's novel engages masterfully, and which, at least to my mind, coincides with the novel's political significance. In a more literal sense, one could actually see how the novelistic writing itself subverts the miniaturist tradition by offering the plot of the novel as an accompanying text to the cluster of illustrations around which the whole action revolves, implying that narratives are always human business with an author, a signature, and an open perspective, regardless of the sacred and otherworldly significations that societies or individuals attach to them. Also, Pamuk, similarly to the murderer, reveals his own signa-ture in the final pages of the text where he appears as one of the narrators, the son of Shekure, who outspokenly confesses that, "for the sake of a delightful and convincing story, there isn't a lie Orhan wouldn't deign to tell."[81] Or, to put it differently, Pamuk desacral-izes the strictly sacred universe of Islam through the theatralization of the Islamic theological and cultural context of the sixteenth century, implying that there is no otherworldly reality that exists outside human experience and understanding.

It also has to be said that the domain of culture shows in practice how the poetic is linked to the political. Because of its performative nature – or as Enishte puts it, "I realize . . . that the meaning has changed and . . . I begin to read the painting anew" – society's ability to imagine and recreate meaning each time anew can never be exhausted in the event of a specific historical realization. Artwork, literary writing, and, generally, works of culture have indispensable historical meaning not only because they point to a specific moment in time – in the case of Pamuk's novel, the encounter between the dogmatic, metaphysical, and retrograde Ottoman world with the humanistic ideals of the European Renaissance – but rather as a testimony to society's imagined non-instrumental otherness. Poesis – regardless of whether we understand it in artistic, social, or political terms – as a force that changes, does not have a precise project that has to be implemented and executed in a particular future; it is limitless, its works are indefinite, and, mostly, it cannot be reduced to its parts precisely because it involves reinvention and re-discovery each time anew. Or, if I refer to Cornelius Castoriadis's socio-political philosophy, poesis, which opens up the possibility for change or self-propelled othering, is another way of understanding the "social-imaginary institution of society." [82] It is also a fundamental condition for democratic life, as Panagia's argument suggests, because the poetic and aesthetic dimensions of political thinking contain "a cluster of potentialities whose actualization has not yet been determined but to which we must remain open."[83]

A Discussion of Divine Heteronomy

The novel opens with the words of the corpse of one of the murdered miniaturists:

> My death conceals an appalling conspiracy against our religion, our traditions and the way we see the world. Open your eyes, discover why the enemies of the life in which you believe, of the life you are living, and of Islam, have destroyed me. Learn why one day they might do the same to you. One by one, everything predicted by the great preacher Nusret Hoja of Erzurum, to whom I've tearfully listened, is coming to pass. Let me say also that if the situation into which we've fallen were described in a book, even the most expert miniaturists could never hope to illustrate it. As with the Koran – God forbid I'm misunderstood – the staggering power of such a book arises from the impossibility of its being depicted.[84]

This opening paragraph contains the greatest dilemma that stays not only at the action center of the novel but is also related to a deeper, almost tragic, and reflectively developed layer pertaining to the clash between, on the one hand, the human will and imagination to create images in different styles and perspectives (and also to participate and navigate the process of self-creation) and, on the other hand, the divine decree of unrepresentability of God Himself and His most sophisticated creations, namely the world and the human being. Therefore, by favoring a homogeneous vision of the world, Eastern miniaturists avoid the depiction of multiple points of view and personal style in order to stick to a strictly dogmatic understanding of seeing, mostly the belief that there is only one way of seeing and it is from Allah's infinite perspective. As the voice of the murderer declares: "It was Satan who first said 'I'; it was Satan who adopted a style!"[85]

The novel, therefore, enters an extremely important theological discussion on the representability of God (the significance of which cannot be fully exhausted in the frames of this analysis). Pamuk resolves some of the dilemmas that come with the attempt at representation of God artistically in a way that revolves around the glorious capacity of human beings to imagine divinity, to invent the principles and codes of submission to it, and, at the same time, to camouflage the act of imagination by not acknowledging the source of creation. It seems that for Pamuk, this is actually a hubristic act equally worthy of discussion, compared to the more traditional understanding of hubris, which is related to human beings' desire to imagine that they are or that they act like Gods. Certainly the substitution of the static, divine-like perspective in a miniature painting with a human-centered, three-dimensional image qualifies as an act of hubris according to the traditional understanding of the term. As it is an act of hubris on the part of Orhan Pamuk to conceal his signature in the novel as if to remind that he is the author of this utterly human masterpiece that quotes from, comments on, and even competes with the divine scripture. And yet, even more perilous and daring than all of this is the establishment of the enigma of God, which is invented to cover the essentially groundless, abysmal existence of human beings: an enigma that is designed to hide human being's tragic finitude. This discussion constitutes an extremely subtle layer in the novel that penetrates the many dimensions of the narrative structure.

The awareness of human beings' tragic finale is certainly presented through the voices of the speaking corpses that reflect on the act of murder and art while at the same time witnessing their own decaying bodies, and also through the voice of Enishte who, after being killed, contemplates from above his whole life realizing that it is just a glimpse of dispersed moments that co-exist simultaneously without any prior logic or direction: "Events I once endured briskly and sequentially were now spread over infinite space and existed simultaneously. As in one of those large double leaf paintings wherein a witty miniaturist has painted a number of unrelated things in each corner – many things were happening all at once."[86] But also, and more importantly, the tragic, Pamuk implies, is deeply inherent to the art forms that have the capacity to simultaneously hide and expose humans' tragic temporality. The only way for art to outmaneuver the tragic dimension of life is either by attaching itself to transcendentalist frameworks (to become religious art as in the case of the Eastern miniatures) or by turning itself into a heteronomous reality (art as an independent world in and of itself as in the case of European romanticism or, generally, the Western tradition discussed en gross in the novel). The true significance, indeed, of miniaturist painting is its relationship to the story narrated and, mostly, to Allah's unchangeable perspective on the world. As Black, for whom calligraphy is the finest form of pure art, reflects in the novel, an individual painting, expressing just an individual style, is disconnected from the story and thus devoid of greater meaning: "by examining such single leaves, you couldn't tell which scene or which story they represented; rather, you would admire it for its own sake, for the pleasure of beholding alone."[87] Being decontextualized, Black suggests, the painting is like an orphaned tree – it has an origin but it does not have a meaning. Art, in order to serve the purpose of higher meaning, must be heteronomous art. It is created in order to invent and imagine a deeper meaning, a coincidence between the world as it is and Allah's perfect design while at the same time camouflaging the apprehension that the human condition might be groundless, un-representable, abysmal, and meaningless at its core.

In the broader and more complicated perspective of the novel as a work of culture, religion itself appears as an epistemological horizon that conceals and substitutes the terms of encounter with the transitoriness of life. Religious art in that respect is a mirror reflecting the creation of religion, not purely as an aesthetic experience but more importantly as a socially effective force that represents, localizes, and navigates (all by concealment) the abyss of human existence. The Eastern miniatures, calligraphy, and the Qur'an itself are material objects but also realities as abstract as the ninety-nine names of God, Satan's speech(es), the sacred text, etc.; each are complex social-imaginary creations that act as sacred items of adoration, almost idolatrous in their signification, whose function is to simulate a way out of the tragic finitude they actually represent by concealing. Therefore, even such abstractions as the sacred words open up a non-representational space for idolatrous worship. Pamuk's intuition here is brilliant because if one follows this interpretation to its limit then the radical monotheistic prescription for prohibition of images, that penetrates the central drama of the novel, becomes meaningless. Religion itself via its various artistic forms is always, against its self-avowed intentions, a representation of the complex human fear of the cosmological abyss. And, as such, it is a human invention very much similar to all other historical forms, which, in the process of secularization, have tried to provide a safe-guard against this basic existential and ontological insecurity: constitutions, nations, ideologies, left and right utopias, among others.

In a different key, this is also another confirmation of the fact that the process of secularization is inexhaustible by definition because it signifies, on the one hand, the desire of liberation from the imposed constraints of religion but also the invention of other safeguards against the encounter with finitude – this encounter is actually an event that has to be constantly staged and relived in various historical situations. The groundlessness of human life cannot be observed once and for all; we cannot just be done with it and move on. In one of the final scenes in the novel, Sultan Ahmed dreams that the Prophet Muhammad denounces the heretical artwork of the infidels and destroys the monumental clockwork organ, itself a fine piece of art and a gift from Queen Elizabeth I. This is a desperate gesture on the side of the religious fundamentalists in the novel to ban the movement of time and, in more abstract terms, to deny the existence of the cosmological abyss that confronts them with a world stripped of any prior exis-tential guarantees.

The prohibition of images in the monotheistic imaginary, to which the strict Islamism belongs (but is not invented by Islam per se – the Hebrew tradition, the early Monophysites, Byzantine icon-oclasm, Protestant asceticism, etc. all have a tradition of image prohibition), includes a narrow definition of image. The ban is against objects that are in direct reference to the divine because they are considered as possessing divine properties and worshipped in themselves as God (or as idols). The actual prohibition, however, is against the very attempt at representation of God, the audacity to give God a form, since it is only God who forms. Or, even more, God is the only agency of form, of which humans are an exemplary byproduct. This is probably the reason why Satan in *My Name is Red* is fascinated with form: "It is not the content but the form of thought that counts. It's not what a miniaturist paints but his style. Yet, these things should be subtle."[88]

The Turkish verb *biçim*,[89] which means "to form" but also "to cut, to shape or hew," seems an appropriate choice here because it has the same meaning as *poiein* (from which the notion of poesis is derived), the Greek word meaning not only the art of making but also the art of forming. The poet, as discussed with regard to Nadeem Aslam's writing, is the one who possesses the power to shape, to form and thus to transform the morals of his or her time. The poet's task is far more complicated than just creating verses. Because this act of forming and transforming is an essentially political task – the creation of otherness is a matter of an immanent process of an open and infinite poesis rather than a transcendental process where otherness appears as an external authority given once and for all – Plato bans the poet from the city.[90] The same destiny is reserved for the miniaturist painters whose desire for a personal style appears as a direct challenge to God's very essence as the supreme agency of form, as the one and only creator who is capable of harnessing an unalterable version of the universe in which an unchangeable version of morality and truth preside over personal or collective doubt. But what is really feared by those who oppose the introduction of perspective is that artistic style contains an element of destruction. It alters the infinite perspective of Allah without providing any guarantee that what comes with the multiple human perspectives on the world has a secure meaning and a stable origin.

The words of Satan intuit the dangers of personal style: "Is man important enough to warrant being drawn in every detail, including his shadow? If the houses in the street were rendered according to man's false perception, that they gradually diminish in size as they recede into the distance, wouldn't man then be effectively usurping Allah's place at the center of the world?"[91] It is, indeed, Pamuk tells us via the image of Satan, an extraordinary hubris to imagine the small, transitory, and historical man taking the place of the omnipotent, ahistorical, and magnificent God. Yet, God and Satan are figures that participate in the same economy of belief, and in *My Name Is Red* their voices are just two perspectives among the many others. At the same time, a phrase from Shekure somehow alludes to the greater stakes that are invested in the rivalry between painting from God's perspective and painting from the perspective of the human being: "A great painter does not content himself by affecting us with his masterpieces; ultimately, he succeeds in changing the landscape of our minds." [92] Imagination, therefore, is a matter of an even more radical audacity because it does not only allow human beings to dethrone God from his central place but it enables them also to imagine God as the single ubiquitous painter of the human world. This particular phantasm is truly magnificent because it envisions an arrangement of the universe prescribed by an agent who is conveniently not available. And it is also a supreme ontological hubris because the radical imagining of God is always accompanied by a denial of the act of imagination, which bars a possible balance of what is gained and what is destroyed in the poetic process.

Conclusion

Beyond the Damaged Notions
of East and West

In a short essay[1] dedicated to one's personal relationship with God, Nadeem Aslam describes how his mother attended one evening a devotional performance of Islamic music. The same evening her brother, his uncle, had become a follower of a strict version of Islam that prohibited such gatherings. When he discovered where his sister was he waited at the front door of their grandparents house for her return, a cane in his hands.

In one of his novels Aslam describes an adult Muslim devotee who took children's toys from them and returned them broken. Islam forbids idolatry. Toys can be considered idols and therefore have to be destroyed. Similarly, the statues of Buddha were dynamited and destroyed in March 2001 after the Taliban government of Afghanistan denounced them as idols. Aslam also described how his uncle one day forcefully took a mask from his small nephew's hands and tore it to pieces. Shock and incomprehension. Later on, he remembers the gradual spread of 'Islamic values' in Pakistan: the Qur'an had to be chanted on the radio and television, children had to be named with archaic Arabic names, criminals were flogged or publicly hanged.

At the same time, there is another image lurking behind: a copy of the Qur'an that is magnificently painted: the lovingly illuminated borders, the geometric designs on the pages where each surah begins, a small chrysanthemum flower instead of a full stop at the end of each verse. Again, in Nadeem Aslam one can read: "Allah will surely prove his love for his creatures by filling Paradise not only with wine and beautiful girls and boys, as promised, but with arabesques as well." The arabesque – containing the amazing beauty of the art of calligraphy . . .

One day Aslam witnessed his uncle becoming enthralled by a small intricate bird folded out of red paper. In a few minutes the uncle regained consciousness and smashed the artificial creature. But for a few moments he had encountered wonder and seen beauty in something he despised, something he went on to destroy . . .

The Western-Islamic public sphere operates inside the secular. The notion *secular* in this book designates the open and infinite process of de-transcendentalization, which means transforming the meta-physical contents in discursive realities. Secularization is a historical process. It names the activity of working on and thus transforming the prevalent theological imaginary. Secularism, by contrast, is an institutional term that pertains less to a process than to a set of definitions that encounter history as a project. Insofar as both religion and secularism claim to be ahistorical frameworks, they are both interested in the re-transcendentalization of history and not in its time-bound dimension. Therefore, the notion of the Western-Islamic public sphere, as I have hopefully shown, is designed to be one possible perspective for dismantling the atemporal, heteronomous (belonging to an un-decidable beyond) theological structures of both dogmatic Islam and dogmatic secularism. The Western-Islamic public sphere is predicated on the idea of critique and it is impossible without the discursive and political practices of critical Muslim intellectuals.

Placing the Qur'an and the whole dogmatic theology of Islam in time and space is semantically linked to the secular. The word *secular*, being etymologically linked with time, does not only involve the gradual retreat of God from the public domain, but it primarily connotes the advent of a common space in which finite human beings negotiate and deliberate the actions of their finite lives. The secular is the historical and its rejection does not only mean the rejection of history and therefore of the ability of human beings to generate change in their social conditions, but also the rejection of religion insofar as the latter is embodied in series of complicated, historically contingent practices and rituals. The intellectual production of the Muslim intellectuals discussed throughout the book does not take a step against Islamic religion as such but, rather, it maintains that its emergence, legitimation, authorization, and canonical execution, in fact its sacredness, is a historical privilege. Precisely because the Qur'an is a historical occurrence, the *arche* and the *telos* of the Islamic social imaginary is determinable.

The major contribution of the book is the introduction and elaboration of the concept of a Western-Islamic public sphere that is currently non-existent in theorizations on religion and the public sphere. Only a nuanced, informed, and attentive approach to the complexities of textual and political practices that involve religion could generate conceptually new tools that would transcend the atemporal, rigid, and heteronomous dogmata of any religious or secularist project. My desire has been to show how the Western-Islamic public sphere is an alternative response to precisely those aspects of religion and public power that tend to employ heteronomous frameworks in defense of their perpetuity. In a sense, the Western-Islamic public sphere is a prism through which tran-scendentalist discourses (regardless of whether religious or secularist) of literalism, exclusion, and dogma should (and can) be exposed and overcome.

Yet, there are at least three bigger research questions that arise as a result of the currently presented work on critical Islam and the Western-Islamic public sphere. The first one is related to an explo-ration of the legitimacy and standing of critical Islam in Muslim-majority countries. In what kind of political projects are critical Muslim intellectuals involved in the world of Islam? In what kind of languages are their messages articulated and from what kind of angles are they criticized for taking a stand against dogmatic reli-gious, state, or military theology as political or existential alternatives to intellectual and state freedom? Those questions are particularly intriguing in the context of the Arab Spring revolutions, which conveyed the reawakening of the Arab world in general and against an increasingly powerless Arab elite; is critical Islam, in this context, a dissident discourse, an imperialist agenda orchestrated by the West, or a cryptic theology that supports the status quo? Does critical Islam exist at all in the Muslim world or, rather, as my research here suggests, it is primarily a Western-born and Western-centered Muslim discourse? A second important question relates to the pragmatics of the Western-Islamic public sphere. As described in the book, the Western-Islamic public sphere is mainly an intel-lectual universe that stems out of the double desire of Western Muslims to fight dogmatism in religion but also to respond in creative, imaginative, yet simultaneously political ways to Western Islamophobia. Yet, a pragmatic question remains to be answered: namely, how exactly do those new Muslims envision an institution-ally grounded political collaboration between Western secular state regimes and Islam? In that respect, a subfield question is where those Muslims look and find institutional support and, mostly, how university departments invested in the study of Islam as the post-colonial 'other' engages the activism of critical Islam.

A third question is generally related to the politics of religion. A comparative perspective between critical Islam and critical discourses in Christianity and Judaism would reveal even further the complexity of what Western Muslim intellectuals are trying to achieve by positioning themselves, similarly to Christian and Judaic scholars prior to them, simultaneously inside the secular and the religious universe. This study should not be restricted only to textual practices but also it should examine in depth the praxis of critique and, more precisely, the fact that seemingly religious individuals strive to become active political agents in completely secular(ist) political environments. Their frameworks of authorizations should be examined more closely, as well as the political projects that stem from them. In that respect, yet again, a case study of the North American appropriation of religious discourse – Christian, Jewish, and, more recently, Islamic – in a secularist state environment is appropriate, especially in the context of the global resurgence of religions and the ongoing American claim to world leadership.

Regardless of the direction in which the research on the Western-Islamic public sphere continues, it is important that the main conceptual horizons that have been introduced here are preserved: namely, the understanding that the conditions of radical (self-)interrogation, or intellectual critique, and uncertainty are actually foundational to political alertness and that without them the parameters of any political decision are questionable. Also, this means that critique and uncertainty generate a sharp focus on the present (as short-lived as the present moment may be) and probably an enormous investment in the future: a future, of course, which is present and not endlessly postponed. In that respect, Edward Said's words that "all criticism is postulated and performed on the assumption that it is to have a future"[2] seem to require simultaneously two incompatible attitudes towards the world: scepticism and utopia. Yet, they are not entirely incompatible because the sceptic warns the utopian to be observant of the present and careful about everything that concerns our common existence and therefore needs to be judged, while the utopian saves the sceptic from the dangers of losing himself into the abyss of the negative. As applied to the Western-Islamic public sphere – a project situated very much in time – this means that the utopic elements in it not only have to be cherished but have to be understood as a work of the present and the sceptic elements in it have to be regarded as the work of what cannot be granted once and for all with any certainty that they are not pure phantasm.

Notes

Introduction: The Damaged Notions of East and West

1   Walter Benjamin, *On the Concept of History*, trans. Dennis Redmond, http://www.marxists.org/reference/archive/benjamin/1940/history. htm

2   For comprehensive commentary on Benjamin's thesis, see Michael Lowy, *Fire Alarm: Reading Walter Benjamin's "On the Concept of History"* (London: Verso, 2006).

3   As observed by Stathis Gourgouris, Marx's eighteenth Brumaire is quite illuminating here: "People make their own history but they do not make it as they please," in Stathis Gourgouris, *"Žižek's Realism,"* in Slavoj *Žižek: The Reality of the Virtual, DVD, produced by Ben Wright (2007; Olive Films)*.

4   Cornelius Castoriadis, *The Imaginary Institution of Society*, trans. Kathleen Blamey (Cambridge, MA: MIT Press, 1998).

5   This equation or, rather, this privilege for political theology is fashionable in social sciences, humanities, and theory nowadays. In a popular commentary on Benjamin, *Žižek* claims that in the context of the postsecular societies in which we live today, "the puppet called theology is to win every time," Slavoj *Žižek, The Puppet and the Dwarf: The Perverse Core of Christianity* (Cambridge, MA: MIT Press, 2003), 3. At the same time, very often the defense of politics is considered anti-imperialist, emancipatory, and anti-colonial; politics – which is extremely important and whose deepest commitments I share at their core – sometimes happens through a subscription to religious dogma or to heteronomous forms of thinking, which some scholars find problematic. On the topic, see Richard Landes, "Judith Butler and the Adorno Prize: A Preliminary Annotated Bibliography," *The Augean Stables,* http://www.theaugeanstables.com/2012/09/13/judith-butler-and-the-adorno-prize-a-preliminary-annotated-bibliography/. The most radical opponent to the heteronomous element in the defense of postcolonial identity politics is Stathis Gourgouris. See his "Antisecularist Failures: A Counterresponse to Saba Mahmood," *Public Culture* 20, no. 3 (2008): 453–459.

6   For a more detailed discussion of the critique against critical Islam, see "Against Heteronomy", p. 19 of this volume.

7 Aamir R. Mufti, "The Aura of Authenticity," *Social Text* 18, no. 3 (2000): 87–88.
8 Most prominent in the debate around recent work on Islam in anthropology and postcolonial studies are Talal Asad and Saba Mahmood: See Saba Mahmood, "Secularism, Hermeneutics and Empire: the Politics of Islamic Reformation," *Public Culture* 18, no. 2 (2006): 323–347; the interviews with Saba Mahmood and Talal Asad in, Nermeen Shaikh, *The Present as History: Critical Perspectives on Contemporary Global Power* (New York: Columbia University Press, 2007), 148–171 & 205–224; the discussion hosted by *The Immanent Frame* on the topic Is Critique Secular? (initially organized around Mahmood's article on Islamic reformation) in *The Immanent Frame*, "Is critique secular?" http://blogs.ssrc.org/tif/category/is-critique-secular/; Talal Asad et al., *Is Critique Secular? Blasphemy, Injury and Free Speech* (Los Angeles: The Townsend Centre for the Humanities, University of California, Berkeley, 2009); and two critical articles on the anthropological work on Islam of Asad and Mahmood, written by the social anthropologist of Islam Sindre Bangstad, "Contesting Secularism/s. Secularism and Islam in the work of Talal Asad," *Anthropological Theory* 9, no. 2 (2009): 188–208 and "Saba Mahmood and Anthropological Feminism after Virtue," *Theory, Culture and Society* 28, no. 3 (May 2011): 28–54.
9 The most recent collection of papers on secularism by renowned experts in the field: Craig Calhoun, Mark Juergensmeyer, and Jonathan Van Antwerpen, eds., *Rethinking Secularism* (Oxford: Oxford University Press, 2011); see especially Jose Casanova, "The Secular, Secularizations, Secularisms," 54–74.
10 The distinction between secularization and secularism is inspired here by the work of William Connolly who, in his book *The Ethos of Pluralization*, distinguishes between the terms pluralism (which equals being and is considered closed and finished) and pluralisation (which equals becoming and is, therefore, an open and unfinished project); William Connolly, *Ethos of Pluralization* (Minnesota: University of Minnesota Press, 1995).
11 Karl Marx, "Introduction to the Contribution to the Critique of Hegel's *Philosophy of Right*," in *Karl Marx, Frederick Engels: Collected Works*, vol. 3, trans. Richard Dixon et al. (New York: International Publishers, 1975), 17. Emphasis in the original.
12 Sheldon Wolin. *Politics and Vision: Continuity and Innovation in Western Political Thought* (Princeton, NJ: Princeton University Press, 2004).
13 Plato, The *Republic: Book X*, trans. Benjamin Jowett, *The Internet Classics Archive*, http://classics.mit.edu/Plato/republic.11.x.html, 595b. See also the fascinating discussion on the intertwinement of

philosophy and poetry: Stanley Rosen, *The Quarrel Between Philosophy and Poetry: Studies in Ancient Thought* (New York: Routledge, 1988), 4.

1 The Politics of Critical Islam

1 Reinhard Koselleck, *The Practice of Conceptual History: Timing History, Spacing Concepts*, trans. Todd Samuel Presner (Stanford: Stanford University Press, 2002), 237.
2 Stathis Gourgouris, "De-transcendentalizing the Secular," *Public Culture* 20, no. 3 (2008): 437–8.
3 Abu Hamid Al-Ghazali, *The Jewels of the Qur'an: Al-Ghazali's Theory*, trans. Muhammad Abul Quasem (Kuala Lumpur: University of Malaysia Press, 1977), 86.
4 For an exhaustive reflection on the Enlightenment notion of reason in relation to Cornelius Castoriadis's "social imaginary" and the psycho-analysis of Lacan and Irigaray see Stathis Gourgouris, "On Self-Alteration," *Parrhesia* 9 (2010), 13–17.
5 Hisam al-Din Ibn Musa Afaneh, "To Hit Students: between Ban and Permissibility," (November 13, 2005), http://www.onislam.net/arabic/ask-the-scholar/8308/8294/52285-2004-08-01%2017-37-04.html; the translated summary is mine. However, I am indebted for this reference to a Bulgarian colleague and a scholar of Medieval Islam, Atanas Shinikov, whose yet unpublished dissertation entitled *To Flog or Not to Flog: What a Question Is It. On Instructive Uses of Violence in Sources of Islamic Pedagogy and Education* explores in depth medieval Sunni sources in which flogging is closely linked to divinely revealed concepts of authority.
6 Ibn Taymiyya, *Fatawa Ibn Taymiyya* (Mansoura: Dar-al-Wafa' li-l-ila'a wal-Nashr, 2005), 274.
7 The complexities of the legal category of punishment as *add* are comprehensively described in Rudolph Peters, *Crime and Punishment in Islamic Law: Theory and Practices from the Sixteenth to the Twenty-first Century* (Cambridge: Cambridge University Press, 2005). See also Christian Lange, *Justice, Punishment and the Medieval Muslim Imagination* (Cambridge: Cambridge University Press, 2008).
8 As one of the most controversial verses of the Qur'an, this passage has been translated numerous times and has been subject to various scholarly discussions. The translation here is by Iraqi-English scholar N.J. Dawood, originally published in 1956 by the Penguin Classics edition of the Qur'an. I am quoting here the revised edition, published in 2008. For alternative translations see J.M Rodwell's (1876), Marmaduke Pickthall's (1922), A.J. Arberry's (1955), M.H. Shakir's (1983), among others. For a critical hermeneutic discussion of the verse, see: Sa'diyya Shaikh, "Exegetical Violence: *Nushuz* in Quranic

Gender Ideology," *Journal for Islamic Studies* 17 (1997): 49–73. See also Kecia Ali, "Understanding a Difficult Verse, Qur'an 4:34," *Sisters in Islam, Empowering Voices for Change,* http://www.sistersinislam. org.my/news.php?item.42.46.

9   This particular hadith has been transmitted in different versions by Abu Dawuud (d. 889), al-Tirmidhi (d. 893), Ibn Majah (d. 887), Ahmad (d. 885), and Ibn Hiban (d. 965). Even though the narration is most probably fabricated, it nonetheless has grave theological, moral, and social consequences. For a thorough analysis of the hadith, see Khaled M. Abou El Fadl, *And God Knows the Soldiers: The Authoritative and the Authoritarian in Islamic Discourse* (Lanham: University Press of America, 2001), 43–82.

10   There is a fatwa on the topic of prostration issued by the Society for Adherence to the Sunnah (SAS). The full text of the fatwa and analysis of its legitimacy is found in El Fadl, *And God Knows the Soldiers*, 43–83.

11   Quoted in El Fadl, *And God Knows the Soldiers*, 128.

12   Those traditions usually depict (with some variations) the Prophet saying, on different occasions, that he has seen in a dream that the women are the majority of the inhabitants in hell. El-Fadl considers those narrations of weak transmission; see El Fadl, *And God Knows the Soldiers*, 129. Also, English translations of the hadiths in question along with instructions on marriage can be found in "Examination of Husband's Rights" in Abu Hamid Al-Ghazali, *Book on the Etiquette of Marriage*, trans. Madelain Farah, http://www.ghazali.org/works/marriage.htm.

13   Abu Hamid Al-Ghazali, Iliyaa Uluum Al-din (Cairo: Daar Al-Me 'rifah), 2:59. A full translation by Madelain Farah is available in the subchapter called "Etiquette for the Woman" in Al-Ghazali, *Book on the Etiquette of Marriage.*

14   For a discussion of Nadeem Aslam's *Maps for Lost Lovers*, see chapter 5.

15   Al-Tabari, Abu Jaafar Muhammad ibn Jarir. *Tafsir al-Tabari'* (Cairo: Maktabat Ibn Taymiyya, no date): 8:290. A brilliant translation and commentary of the passage is also found in Atanas Shinikov, *To Flog or Not to Flog: What a Question Is It. On Instructive Uses of Violence in Sources of Islamic Pedagogy and Education* (PhD diss., Sofia University St. Kliment Ohridski).

16   See a discussion of those hadith traditions in El Fadl, *And God Knows the Soldiers*, 68–69.

17   Qur'an, 74:31. My translation.

18   On the theological, ethical, and legal complexities of the Islamic normative framework, see Muhammad Fadel, "Muslim Reformists, Female Citizenship and the Public Accommodation of Islam in Liberal Democracy," in *Politics and Religion* (Cambridge: Cambridge

University Press, 2012), http://ssrn.com/abstract=1727457. See also Muhammad Fadel, "The True, the Good and the Reasonable: the Theological and Ethical Roots of Public Reason in Islamic Law," *Canadian Journal of Law and Jurisprudence* 21, no. 1 (2008): 21–29 and 67.

19 El Fadl, *And God Knows the Soldiers*, 20–21.

20 Ebrahim Moosa, "The Debts and Burdens of Critical Islam," in *Progressive Muslims: On Justice, Gender and Pluralism*, ed. Omid Safi (Oxford: One World Publications, 2003), 111–127.

21 Ebrahim Moosa, "The Debts and Burdens of Critical Islam," 114.

22 Qur'an, 6:165; translated by Pickthall.

23 Qur'an, 35:38–39; translated by Pickthall.

24 For the ethical implications of Islamic transcendentalism, see John Morgan, "Beyond Ethical Theism: Islamic morality as a service to God," *Contemporary Islamic Studies. A Qatar Foundation Academic Journal* (May 2011): 1–5.

25 For this branch of historical study, see Cornelius Castoriadis, *The Imaginary Institution of Society*, 195–210.

26 This, in a sense, is something that Nancy suggests. However, his text tracing the separation between the state and religion while affirming the impossibility of the classical secularist narrative suddenly undermines the historical register he initially adopts. The state, which Nancy at a certain point identifies with the embodiment of the political, as *being-in-common*, is multi-referential in history (it is not only a category of thinking, as Nancy himself admits); while precisely the philosophical register, in the second part of the article, he disposes with reductions of the historical multiplicity to abstract categories. The 'state' and 'being-in-common,' in that regard, are notions that belong to different reflexive registers. "The other as a wound to my own being" and "the horror of solitude" are figures hardly sensible to the historical grammars of the political, concerned, foremost, with the intertwinement of the legal, the social, the ethical, and the individual inside the public sphere. As compromised as it might be, the notion "public sphere" is still, it seems to me, very pertinent to the conceptualization of the political as a space of being together. See, Jean-Luc Nancy, "Church, State, Resistance," in *Political Theologies: Public Religions in a Post-Secular World*, ed. Hent de Vries and Lawrence E. Sullivan (New York: Fordham University Press, 2006), 110–11.

27 The terms autonomy and heteronomy are employed here in the Kantian sense where heteronomous will means obedience to rules of action that have been legislated externally to it, whereas autonomous will is entirely self-legislative. Despite the fact that in the book I rethink the Kantian mechanisms of achieving autonomy, I remain faithful throughout to his understanding of the two notions. See Immanuel

Kant, *Groundwork of the Metaphysics of Morals*, trans. H.J. Paton (New York: Harper & Row, 1964), 58.

28 For a commentary on Arkoun's and Zayd's hermeneutical projects and Benslama's psychoanalytic project, see chapter 2. For a further commentary on Fethi Benslama's psychoanalysis of Islam, see Dilyana Mincheva, "'Critical Islam': Debating/Negotiating Modernity," *Journal of Religion and Society* 14 (2012): paragraphs 28–35, http://moses.creighton.edu/jrs/2012/2012-18.pdf.

29 Those studies are usually doubly inspired by the Foucauldian critique of power that builds the theoretical armature of Said's *Orientalism* and by the polemical stance in the Saidian text against classical orientalism, which caricatures Islam for being irrational, violent, and uncivilized. See, Talal Asad, *Genealogies of Religion: Discipline and Reason of Power in Christianity and Islam* (Baltimore: The Johns Hopkins University Press, 1993) and Talal Asad, *Formations of the Secular: Christianity, Islam, Modernity* (Stanford: Stanford University Press, 2003). See also a collection of articles dedicated to Asad's anti-secularism: David Scott and Charles Hirschkind, eds., *Powers of the Secular Modern: Talal Asad and His Interlocutors* (Stanford: Stanford University Press, 2006). See also chapter 3 of the current book.

30 Edward Said, *The World, the Text and the Critic* (Cambridge, MA: Harvard University Press, 1983), 35.

31 Said, *The World, the Text and the Critic*, 29. For a thorough examination of Said's understanding of the secular, see Mathieu Courville, *Edward Said's Rhetoric of the Secular* (London: Continuum, 2010).

32 Talal Asad, "Historical Notes on the Idea of Secular Criticism," in *The Immanent Frame: Secularism, Religion and the Public Sphere* (blog), 25 January 2008, http://blogs.ssrc.org/tif/2008/01/25/historical-notes-on-the-idea-of-secular-criticism/

33 See Charles Taylor, *A Secular Age* (Cambridge, MA: Belknap Press of Harvard University Press, 2007).

34 The question is originally formulated by Stathis Gourgouris in a theoretical discussion on the identity and future of comparative literature as a secular interdisciplinary field of research. See Stathis Gourgouris, "The *Poiein* of Secular Criticism," in *A Companion to Comparative Literature*, ed. Ali Behdad and Dominic Thomas (West Sussex, UK: Wiley-Blackwell, 2011), 83–86.

35 Gourgouris, "The *Poiein* of Secular Criticism," 84.

36 Joseph Ratzinger and Jürgen Habermas, *The Dialectics of Secularization: On Reason and Religion* (San Francisco: Ignatius Press, 2007), 55–57.

37 Benedict Anderson, *Imagined Communities: Reflection on the Origin and Spread of Nationalism* (London: Verso, 2006).

38 Jürgen Habermas, *Structural Transformations of the Public Sphere,*

trans. Thomas Burger with the assistance of Frederic Lawrence (Cambridge, MA: MIT Press, 1991).

39 An interesting article, on the topic of radical imagination, by Anthony Bogus outlines two types of imagination. The first type is related to the Kantian notion of "reproductive function" and it works to create and reinforce hegemony. The second type, however, is what Bogus defines as imagination that operates as critical thought. Here the work of the imagination consists in breaking the boundaries and status quo of everyday life and, effectively, in conjuring what a different world would be like. Or, as Franz Fanon puts it (quoted by Bogus), imagination consists in "introducing invention into existence." See Anthony Bogus, "And What About the Human?: Freedom, Human Emancipation, and the Radical Imagination," *Boundary 2* 39, no. 3 (2012): 44–45.

40 Similar questions in the secular-postsecular debate were originally raised by Stathis Gourgouris in "The *Poiein* of Secular Criticism," 82.

41 Hannah Arendt, *The Origins of Totalitarianism* (Orlando: Benediction Books, 2009).

2 Critical Islam inside the Academia

1 In a post-revolutionary Egypt, a number of intellectuals working at the American University of Cairo are trying to rehabilitate Zayd's scholarly reputation; for one example of this enterprise, see Emran El-Badawi, "Nasr Hamid Abu Zayd: A Film Screening at AUC," *Iqlid*, http://iqlid.wordpress.com/2013/02/18/nhazauc/

2 For an introduction to Muhammed Arkoun's professional biography and the debates that he participated in actively throughout the years, see The Centre for Islamic Sciences, "Muhammed Arkoun," http://cis-ca.org/voices/a/arkoun.htm

3 Stanley Rosen, *Hermeneutics as Politics* (New York: Oxford University Press, 1987), 161.

4 A Pakistani scholar with an Oxford degree, Fazlur Rahman (1919–1988) is considered the pioneer of the field of Quranic hermeneutics. His famous followers are the American-based South-African scholar Ebrahim Moosa and the Iranian scholar in exile Abdel Karim Soroush. Nasr Abu Zayd and Mohammad Arkoun are intellectual heirs to the same tradition of thinking. For introduction to the field, see Victoria S. Harrison, "Hermeneutics, Religious Language and the Qur'an," *Islam and Christian–Muslim Relations* 21, no. 3 (July 2010): 207–220.

5 Abdel Karim Soroush, "Text in Context," *Liberal Islam: a sourcebook*, ed. Charles Kurzman (New York: Oxford, Oxford University Press, 1998), 244–251, http://nawaat.org/portail/2005/02/02/text-in-context-abdolkarim-soroush/

6 Nasr Abu Zayd, "The Qur'an: God and Man in Communication" (Inaugural Lecture, 27 November 2000), *Leiden University, Repository*,
   http://www.let.leidenuniv.nl/forum/01_1/onderzoek/lecture.pdf

7 The Mut'azilite thinkers believed in divine unity and divine justice and tried to combine them with divine omnipotence. This, however, led them to the denial of divine freedom; to save divine justice and unity they had to argue that God's will was eternal and it was also just. God thus could not save whomever He wanted, but had to save all who acted justly. The dominant theological school of the Ash'arites reacted with distrust towards this formulation. The Ash'arites and Hanbalites considered God's omnipotence locked in His ability to will just and unjust acts; actually all acts are morally neutral and they acquire their value only by being willed by God. The philosophy of Ghazali, developed in Baghdad in the eleventh century, marked further the radical break of Islamic theology with rationalism. Ghazali emphasized the absolute alterity of Allah through the concept of a supreme, powerful God. Man, for Ghazali, was a slave to God but he could also be his regent on Earth. This extreme position actually rejected all independence of human beings from divine will. In the theological-philosophical realm, these are precisely the formulations that critical Islam attempts to revisit. For a comprehensive study of Mut'azilism, see J.R.T.M. Peters, *God Created Speech: Study in the Speculative Theology of the Mu'tazili qadi I-qudat Abu-l-Hasan abd Al-Jabar ibn Ahmad al-Hamadani* (The Netherlands: Brill Academic Publishers, 1976). For Abu Zayd's relationship to Mut'azilite philosophy, see Nasr Abu Zayd, "The Dilemma of the Literary Approach to the Qur'an," *Alif: Journal of Comparative Poetics* 23 (2003): 35–40. See, also, the most distinguished scholar in classical Muslim theology, Josef van Ess, *The Flowering Muslim Theology*, trans. Jane Marie Todd (Cambridge, MA: Harvard University Press, 2006), 79–117 (on the Mut'azilite philosophy).

8 Zayd, "The Qur'an: God and Man in Communication," 4.

9 Stathis Gourgouris traces the genealogy of the term in (his) "De-transcendentalizing the Secular," 444.

10 Reza Aslan, *Not God but God* (New York: Random House Trade Paperback Editions, 2006), 70.

11 Aslan, *Not God but God*, 70.

12 The original in Arabic could be roughly translated in this way: *God created spouses for you of your own kind so that you may have peace of mind through them*. See Aslan, *Not God but God*, 69. Another highly respected translation is suggested by Sahih International: "And of His signs is that He created for you from yourselves mates that you may find tranquillity in them; and He placed between you affection and

mercy. Indeed in that are signs for a people who give thought" (http://quran.com/30/21).

13 Quoted in Nathalie Szerman, "Tunisian Reformist Abdelwahab Meddeb: It's Up to the Arab to Take the Courageous Step of Questioning His Faith," in *Arab Watch for Reformation and Democracy* (electronic portal), January 24 2007, http://www.awrd.net/look/en-article.tpl?IdLanguage=1&IdPublication=1&NrArticle=1570&NrIssue=2&NrSection=6

14 Abdelwahab Meddeb, "La burqa est absente de Qur'an," *Nouvel Observateur*, January 28 2010, http://tempsreel.nouvelobs.com/actualite/societe/20100128.OBS5145/la-burqa-est-absente-du-coran.html; (my translation).

15 Muhammed Arkoun, *Islam: To Reform or to Subvert* (London: Saqi Books, 2006), 95.

16 Muhammed Arkoun, "Rethinking Mediterranean Space," *Diogene Unesco* 206 (2004); Arkoun explains the distinction between "Quranic fact" and "Islamic fact" in *Islam: To Reform or to Subvert*, 86–98 and 272–297. See also Muhammed Arkoun, *Rethinking Islam: Common Questions, Uncommon Answers*, trans. and ed. Robert D. Lee (Colorado: Westview Press, 1994), 35–40.

17 One such verse that mentions the effect of recitation and emphasizes the uniqueness of God is 39:23. It says, "Allah has sent down the best statement: a consistent Book wherein is reiteration. The skins shiver therefrom of those who fear their Lord; then their skins and their hearts relax at the remembrance of Allah. That is the guidance of Allah by which He guides whom He wills. And one whom Allah leaves astray – for whom there is no guide"; Translation is mine.
See (Sahih International) http://quran.com/39.23; Arkoun, *Islam: To Reform or to Subvert*, 280.

18 Arkoun, *Islam: To Reform or to Subvert*, 325.

19 Arkoun, *Islam: To Reform or to Subvert*, 332.

20 In this lecture, which triggered the protest of many Muslims – intellectuals and ordinary people, the Pope is recorded pronouncing the following mischaracterization of Islam: "Show me just what Muhammad brought that was new and there you will find things only evil and inhuman, such as his command to spread by the sword the faith he preached," *BBC News*, "Pope Sorry for Offending Muslims," *BBC News*, September 17 2006, http://news.bbc.co.uk/2/hi/europe/5353208.stm

21 Abdelwahab Meddeb, quoted in Michael Mönninger, "Islam's Heritage of Violence," *Die Ziet*, trans. Nicolas Grindell, September 21 2006, http://www.signandsight.com/features/978.html

22 Ruth Mas, "Love as Difference: The Politics of Love in the Thought of Malek Chebel," *European Review of History* 11, no. 2 (2004): 275.

23 Mas, "Love as Difference," 280.
24 Fethi Benslama, *Psychoanalysis and the Challenge of Islam*, trans. Robert Bonnono (Minneapolis: University of Minnesota Press, 2009), 125.
25 See http://www.tariqramadan.com.
26 Tariq Ramadan, "Radical reform: ethics and liberation," http://www.tariqramadan.com/article.php3?id_article=1242& lang=en
27 Tariq Ramadan, "Ce que je crois: le dernier livre de Tariq Ramadan," http://oumma.com/spip.php?article976
28 Armando Salvatore, "Authority in Question: Secularity, Republicanism, and 'Communitarianism' in the Emerging Euro-Islamic Public Sphere," *Theory, Culture and Society* 24, no. 2, 140–141.
29 Mas, "Love as Difference," 282.
30 Tariq Ramadan, *To Be a European Muslim* (Leicester: Islamic Foundation, 1999), 182.
31 Tristan Walleckx, "Naissance médiatique de l'intellectuel musulman en France (1989–2005)," (MA Thesis, Université Montpellier 3, 2005), http://www.memoireonline.com/12/05/63/m_naissance-intel-lectuel-musulman-medias-francais2.html
32 This whole categorization is an artificial construct developed for the needs of various analyses. A comprehensive study of the methods that legitimize it can be found in Walleckx, (see the previous note).
33 Malik Chebel, *L'imaginaire Arabo-Musulman* (Paris: Presses universitaires de France, 1993), 306.
34 Malik Chebel, *Enciclopedie de l'amour en Islam: érotisme, beauté, sexualité dans le monde arabe, en Perse et en Turquie* (Paris: Edition Payot, 1995), 32.
35 Quoted in Mas, "Love as Difference," 288.
36 Benslama, *Psychoanalysis and the Challenge of Islam*, 104–105.
37 Benslama, *Psychoanalysis and the Challenge of Islam*, 125–126.
38 Benslama, *Psychoanalysis and the Challenge of Islam*, 132.
39 Benslama, *Psychoanalysis and the Challenge of Islam*, 274–276.
40 Fethi Benslama, "The Veil of Islam," *Journal of the Jan Van Eyck Circle for Lacanian Ideology Critique* 2 (2009): 16.
41 Benslama, "The Veil of Islam," 24.
42 For an interesting psychoanalytical discussion on the constitution of the subject outside the confines of the Kantian framework, see Gourgouris, "On Self-Alteration," 1–17.
43 The concept of bringing back God at the human centre belongs to Ernst Bloch; see Ernst Bloch, *The Principle of Hope*. Vol. 1, 2, 3 (Cambridge, MA: MIT Press, 1995).
44 Gourgouris, "On Self-Alteration," 13.

3 North-American Post-Colonial Studies and European Polemics against Islam

1 Saba Mahmood, *Politics of Piety: The Islamic Revival and the Feminist Subject* (Princeton and Oxford: Princeton University Press, 2005).

2 Mahmood, "Secularism, Hermeneutics and Empire," 353–367.

3 For a comprehensive analysis and critique of Ramadan's intellectual heritage and thinking, see Paul Berman, *The Flight of the Intellectuals* (Brooklyn, New York: Melville House, 2010).

4 Pascal Bruckner, *The Tyranny of Guilt: An Essay on Western Masochism*, trans. Steven Randall (Princeton: Princeton University Press, 2010), 134.

5 Bruckner, *The Tyranny of Guilt*, 145.

6 Bruckner, *The Tyranny of Guilt*, 154.

7 Bruckner, *The Tyranny of Guilt*, 32.

8 Gourgouris, "Antisecularist Failures," 454.

9 Mahmood, "Secularism, Hermeneutics and Empire," 323–332 esp. 328.

10 Asad, *Formations of the Secular*.

11 Saba Mahmood, "Secular Imperatives," *Public Culture* 20, no. 3 (2008): 462.

12 Gourgouris, "Antisecularist Failures," 455.

13 Mahmood, "Secularism, Hermeneutics and Empire," 336.

14 Mahmood, "Secularism, Hermeneutics and Empire," 337.

15 Mahmood, *Politics of Piety*, 58 and 153–188.

16 Bruckner, *The Tyranny of Guilt*, 12.

17 Pascal Bruckner, *The Tears of the White Man: Compassion as Contempt*, trans. William. R. Beer (New York: The Free Press Division, A Division of Macmillan Inc., 1986), esp. 9–37 and 77–110.

18 Bruckner, *The Tears of the White Man*, 115–138.

19 Bruckner, *The Tyranny of Guilt*, 33–34.

20 Berman, *The Flight of the Intellectuals*, 272.

21 Bruckner, *The Tyranny of Guilt*, 48.

22 Bruckner, *The Tyranny of Guilt*, 53.

23 Pascal Bruckner, "Enlightenment Fundamentalism or the Racism of the Anti-racist," *Signandsight.com: Let's talk European*, 24 January 2007, http://www.signandsight.com/features/1146.html

24 Bruckner, "Enlightenment Fundamentalism."

25 Bruckner, "Enlightenment Fundamentalism"; the article referred to is Timothy Garton Ash, "Islam in Europe," *New York Review of Books*, October 5, 2006, http://www.nybooks.com/articles/archives/2006/oct/05/islam-in-europe/

26 Bruckner, "Enlightenment Fundamentalism."

27 Mahmood, "Secularism, Hermeneutics and Empire," 325.

28 Ayaan Hirsi Ali, *Nomad* (Toronto: Vintage Canada, 2011), Introduction, xviii.
29 Bruckner, *The Tyranny of Guilt*, 218.

4 Literary Voices Turned Political

1 Quoted in Abdelwahab Meddeb, "Human Rights, Divine Rights," (Conference Paper) *Universality of Human Rights Forum, Oslo 21–22 October 2010*, http://forumoslo.fede.org/textes/en/Abdelwahab Meddeb_Human_rights_DivineRight_EN.pdf

2 Nasr Abu Zayd, *Reformation of Islamic Thought: A Critical Historical Analysis* (Amsterdam: Amsterdam University Press, 2006), 98–99.

3 Abdelwahab El-Effendi, "The People on the Edge: Religious Reform and the Burden of Western Muslim Intellectual," *Harvard Middle Eastern and Islamic Review* 8 (2009): 19–50.

4 The one-hour debate could be followed at *Alterinfo*, "Ramadan vs Meddeb 'Collatéral ''Pourquoi, désormais, on ne peut plus discuter avec Abdelwahab Meddeb (vidéo du débat sur de FR3)," *Alterinfo.com*, February 3 2008, http://www.alterinfo.net/Ramadan-vs-Meddeb-Collateral-Pourquoi-desormais-on-ne-peut-plus-discute r-avec-Abdelwahab-Meddeb-video-du-debat-sur-de_a16466.html

5 A kind of reductive reading of Meddeb's critique through a hasty alliance with orientalism is available in Carine Bourget, "9/11 and the Affair of the Muslims Headscarf in Essays by Tahar Ben Jelloun and Abdelwahab Meddeb," *French Cultural Studies* 19 (2008): 71–84; for a commentary on the limitations of the orientalist interpretations, see Chapter 3.

6 James Kidd, "Nadeem Aslam. Interview," *Asia Literary Review* 11 (Spring 2009), http://www.asialiteraryreview.com/web/article/en/24

7 Kidd, "Nadeem Aslam. Interview."

8 On the literary entanglements of politics and poetics, see Gourgouris, "The *Poiein* of Secular Criticism," 84–85.

9 On the complex relationship between politics and literature, see John Fekete, "Literature and Politics/ Literary Politics," *Dalhousie Review* 66, nos. 1–2 (1986): 45–86.

10 See Davide Panagia, *The Political Life of Sensation* (Duke University Press, 2009).

11 Panagia, *The Political Life of Sensation*, 3.

12 Tariq Ramadan's reformation theology has often been suspected of cryptic fundamentalism. Part of the reason is his ties with the founder of the Egyptian branch of the Muslim Brotherhood, Hassan Al-Banna, who is Ramadan's grandfather. For the Ramadan-Meddeb intense exchange of arguments on the reformation of Islam in the French public sphere, see Dilyana Mincheva, "Western Muslim Intellectuals in Dialogue with Secularism: From Religion to Social Critique," *The*

International Journal of Religion and Spirituality in Society 2, no. 1 (2012): 13–24.

13 Abdelwahab Meddeb, "Islam and Its Discontents: An Interview with Frank Berberich," trans. Pierre Joris, *October 99* (Winter 2002): 3–20.

14 Meddeb, "Islam and Its Discontents," 5.

15 Adbelwahab Meddeb, *The Malady of Islam*, trans. Pierre Joris and Anne Reid (New York: Basic Books, 2003), 6–7.

16 See "Fundamentalism against the West," in Meddeb, *The Malady of Islam*, 93–144.

17 Ramadan, *Radical Reform*, 61–77. See also Tariq Ramadan, *Islam, the West and the Challenge of Modernity* (London: The Islamic Foundation, Tra Edition, 2009).

18 For a comprehensive discussion of Tariq Ramadan's ideas, see chapter 2; for a discussion of Al-Ghazal's philosophy, see chapter 4.

19 Abdelkebir Khatibi, *La blessure de nom propre* (Paris: Édition Denoël, 1986), 199; the translation is mine. The original text in French is «Entre le pouvoir et la lettre s'inscrit notre histoire récente (personnelle et nationale). Si cette blessure traduit une actualité trop aveuglante, elle masque en même temps la difficulté, l'immense difficulté, de penser le concept d'histoire.»

20 Abdelwahab Meddeb, *Phantasia* (Paris: Sindbad, 1986), 118. The translation is mine. The original text in French is: «Afin de dérober le sol sous l'œil torve des agités qui occupent les territoires politiques d'islam, il serait convenable de travailler à rendre celui-ci intérieur à l'Europe. Cela le parerait d'une dignité qui aurait l'aura de l'universel.»

21 Dina Al-Kassim, "The Faded Bond: Calligraphesis and Kinship in Abdelwahab Meddeb's *Talismano*," *Public Culture* 13, no. 1 (2001): 115.

22 Meddeb quoted in Samia Mehrez, "Translation and the Postcolonial Experience: the Francophone North-African Text," in *Rethinking Translation*, ed. Lawrence Venuti (London: Routledge, 1992), 124.

23 Abdelwahab Meddeb, "Pourquoi Ecrivez-Vous," *Libération* special issue (March, 1985): p. 112; the translation is mine. The original French text is as follows: «J'écris, hanté par la main dont je fus amputé dans ma vie antérieure, quand j'exerçais la fonction de scribe chez un vizir persan. . . . J'avais inventé un style où la forme avec le nombre s'accorde. Mon maître jaloux m'accusa de rapine et me denonça à la loi; il me fit couper la main. De retour à la vie, mille ans après, je grandis sur les rives d'Afrique. Je m'étais initié aux arcanes de l'exile occidentale, avant de séjourner sous des cieux obscurs. Là, je traduis de mémoire la voix de l'ange que je transcris dans la langue étrangère pour conjurer l'amputation atavique et rééduquer ma main, qui remue come greffe indocile, à la réminiscence du billot maculé de mon sang, tranchante frappe du bourreau, qui m'avait jeté dans l'inconscience,

le bras en deuil, moignon orphelin de cette main qui cogne, griffe, saisit, griffe, donne, caresse, qui, quand elle écrit rassemble en un seul geste tous les échanges dont elle est capable.»

24 Abdelwahab Meddeb, *Talismano* (Paris: Christian Bourgois, 1979), 115; the translation is mine. Here is the French original: «Ma première querelle avec le père éclata mélange des mots pendant la transmission récitative du texte.»

25 Meddeb, *Phantasia,* 58.

26 Meddeb, *Phantasia,* 58; the translation is mine. Here is the French original: «Nul ne mérite à ce que cette vérité ait de fournir sa preuve dans l'authenticité de l'histoire. C'est une mythologie qui est éprouvée par la langue.»

27 Bourget, "9/11 and the Affair of the Muslim Headscarf," 71.

28 Meddeb, *The Malady of Islam,* 18.

29 Bourget, "9/11 and the Affair of the Muslim Headscarf," 78.

30 Meddeb, *The Malady of Islam,* 118–119.

31 Meddeb, *The Malady of Islam,* 117–118.

32 Ali Eteraz, *Children of Dust: A Portrait of a Muslim as a Young Man* (New York: HarperOne, 2009), Prologue.

33 Eteraz, *Children of Dust,* 158.

34 Eteraz, *Children of Dust,* 220.

35 The Holy Qur'an, 5:32; my translation.

36 Eteraz, *Children of Dust,* p. 333.

37 Allison Jones, "All 3 Guilty in Shafia Murder Trial; Judge Condemns Twisted Concept of Honour," *The Canadian Press,* January 30 2012, http://ca.news.yahoo.com/shafia-jury-enters-second-full-day-deliber-ations-kingston-090532874.html

38 Marianne Brace, "Nadeem Aslam: a Question of Honour," *The Independent,* June 11 2004, http://www.independent.co.uk/arts-enter-tainment/books/features/nadeem-aslam-a-question-of-honour-61678 58.html

39 Kidd, "Nadeem Aslam. Interview."

40 Gourgouris, "The *Poiein* of Secular Criticism," 78–79.

41 *Timeous of Plato, In Five Books, Containing a Treasury of Pythagoric and Platonic Physiology,* vol. 1, trans. Thomas Taylor (London: Walworth, Surrey, 1820), 271–272.

42 Nadeem Aslam, *Maps for Lost Lovers* (London: Faber and Faber, 2004), 334.

43 Quoted in James Procter, "A Portrait of Nadeem Aslam," *British Council Literature,* http://literature.britishcouncil.org/nadeem-aslam

44 Aslam, *Maps for Lost Lovers,* 25.

45 Aslam, *Maps for Lost Lovers,* 13.

46 Aslam, *Maps for Lost Lovers,* 213.

47 Aslam, *Maps for Lost Lovers,* 176.

48 Aslam, *Maps for Lost Lovers*, 223.

49 Even though the Qur'an is silent on honour killings, the punishment
    for adultery through stoning and the sanction of murder of adulterous
    men and women exists in the Sunnah of Islam. A famous hadith in one
    of the most authoritative collections, Sahih Muslim, Book 17, hadith
    number 4206, tells the story of a woman who sought through the
    Prophet Muhammad divine punishment for being adulterous. After
    Muhammad took care of the illicit child born out of the sin of this
    woman, he prescribed that she was put in a ditch up to her chest and
    stoned by the community. A translation of the whole hadith is avail-
    able at Sahih Muslim, http://www.hadithcollection.com/ sahihmuslim/
    145-Sahih%20Muslim%20Book%2017.%20 Punishments%20
    Prescribed%20By%20Islam/12549-sahih-muslim-book-017-hadith-
    number-4206.html

50 Quoted in Pankaj Mishra, "The Wilderness of Solitude," *New York
    Review of Books*, June 23 2005, http://www.nybooks.com/articles/
    archives/2005/jun/23/the-wilderness-of-solitude/?pagination=false.

51 These statistics are available through the international data portal on
    honour crimes: http://www.stophonourkillings.com/?q=taxonomy/
    term/168. See also an extensive study on honour killings in Jacqueline
    Rose, "A Piece of White Silk," *London Review of Books* 31, no. 21
    (November 5, 2009), http://www.lrb.co.uk/v31/n21/jacqueline-
    rose/a-piece-of-white-silk

52 Quoted in Brace, "Nadeem Aslam: a Question of Honour."

53 Aslam, *Maps for Lost Lovers*, 348.

54 Quoted in Michael Friscolani, "At the Shafia Honour Trial the Verdict
    Is In: Guilty," *McLean Magazine*, January 29, 2012,
    http://www2.macleans.ca/2012/01/29/shafia-family-found-guilty/

55 Quoted in Friscolani, "At the Shafia Honour Trial."

56 Aslam, *Maps for Lost Lovers*, 348.

57 Aslam, *Maps for Lost Lovers*, 41.

58 Aslam, *Maps for Lost Lovers*, 161.

59 Aslam, *Maps for Lost Lovers*, 312.

60 Aslam, *Maps for Lost Lovers*, 312.

61 For a discussion of Bruckner's essay, see chapter 3.

62 The Holy Father, "Faith, Reason and the University – Memories and
    Reflections," (Lecture) Liberia Editrice Vaticana, September 12,
    2006, http://www.vatican.va/holy_father/benedict_xvi/speeches/
    2006/september/documents/hf_ben-xvi_spe_20060912_university-
    regensburg_en.html; in fact, those words do not belong originally to
    the Pope but they are a quotation from the fourteenth-century
    Byzantine Emperor Manuel Paleologus. The original text of the
    quotation is available in French translation in Adel Theodore Khoury,

Manuel II Paléologue, Entretien avec un Musulman (7e Controverse)
(Paris: Les Edition de Cerf, 1966).

63 Joseph Lumbard, *Submission, Faith and Beauty: the Religion of Islam*
(Louisville, KY: Fons Vitae, 2009).

64 Quoted in Gregory Wolfe, "East and West in Miniature," *Image* 53
(Spring 2007): 1.

65 Nobelprize.org, "The Nobel Prize in Literature 2006," *Nobelprize.org*,
http://www.nobelprize.org/nobel_prizes/literature/laureates/2006/

66 Full bibliographical details could be found about Pamuk on his
website: http://www.orhanpamuk.net/biography.aspx

67 Pamuk is often compared to Salman Rushdie and thus qualified as a
postmodern novelist. Ian Almond defines Pamuk as one of the "new
orientalists" for his critical engagements with Islam: Ian Almond, *The
New Orientalists. Postmodern Representations of Islam from Foucault to
Baudrillard* (New York: I.B. Tauris, 2007), esp. "Islam and
Melancholy in Orhan Pamuk's *The Black Book*," 110–130.

68 The Borzoi Reader Online, "A Conversation with Orhan Pamuk,"
Randomhouse.com, May 2008, http://www.randomhouse.com/knopf/
authors/pamuk/qna.html

69 Plenty of information is available on the internet on the 2005–2006
trial against Orhan Pamuk, which was closely supervised and acutely
condemned by the European institutions in view of Turkey's candi-
dature for membership in the European Union. See Ifex,
"International PEN Calls for Government Condemnation of attacks
on author Orhan Pamuk," *Ifex*, April 6, 2005,
http://www.ifex.org/turkey/2005/04/06/international_pen_calls_for_g
overnment/; Musa Kesler, "Nobel Laureate Orhan Pamuk Gets
Fined," *Hurriyet Daily News*, March 27, 2011, http://www.hurriyet-
dailynews.com/default.aspx?pageid=438&n=orhan-pamuk-will-pay-
compensation-for-his-words-court-decided-2011-03-27; Sarah
Rainsford, "Authors Trial Set to Test Turkey," *BBC News Istanbul*,
December 15, 2005, http://news.bbc.co.uk/2/hi/europe/4527318.stm;
The Guardian, "Trial of Turkish Author Adjourned," *The Guardian*,
December 16, 2005, http://www.guardian.co.uk/world/2005/dec/16/
turkey.books

70 Orhan Pamuk, *My Name Is Red*, trans. Erda Göknar (London: Faber
and Faber, 2001), 79.

71 At the same time, the supremacy of the word over image in the Islamic
tradition is particularly important. It is related to theological prescriptions. This is the reason why calligraphy – which paints images with
words – is considered the most powerful Islamic art. See Thomas
Arnold, *Painting in Islam: A Study of the Pictorial Art in Muslim Culture*
(New York: Dover, 1965), 10.

72 Feride Çiçekoğlu, "A Pedagogy of Two Ways of Seeing: A

Confrontation of "Word and Image in *My Name is Red*," *The Journal of Aesthetic Education* 37, no. 3 (Fall 2003): 4.

73   Pamuk, *My Name Is Red*, 96.

74   Pamuk, *My Name Is Red*, 325.

75   Pamuk, *My Name Is Red*, 489.

76   A literary discussion of *My Name Is Red* as a masterpiece is available in Esra Almas, "Framing *My Name Is Red*: Reading a Masterpiece," in *Global Perspectives on Orhan Pamuk: Existentialism and Politics,* ed. Mehnaz M. Afridi and David M. Buyze (New York: Palgrave Macmillan, 2012), 75–90. My own analysis departs from Esra's literary reading of the novel inasmuch as it aims to discover the mythopoetical mechanisms of Pamuk's writing as related to wider and complex processes of social-historical poiesis, present in the text but ultimately going beyond it.

77   Sadia Abbas, "Leila Aboulela, Religion and the Challenge of the Novel," *Contemporary Literature* 52, no. 3 (Fall 2011): 430–461.

78   Pamuk, *My Name Is Red*, 173.

79   Pamuk, *My Name Is Red*, 168.

80   Davide Panagia, *The Poetics of Political Thinking* (Durham: Duke University Press, 2006), 8.

81   Pamuk, *My Name Is Red*, 413.

82   Castoriadis, *The Imaginary Institution of Society*, 165–215 and 340–369.

83   Panagia, *The Poetics of Political Thinking*, 123.

84   Pamuk, *My Name Is Red*, 5–6.

85   Pamuk, *My Name Is Red*, 287.

86   Pamuk, *My Name Is Red*, 177.

87   Pamuk, *My Name Is Red*, 55.

88   Pamuk, *My Name Is Red*, 291.

89   See translation in Barish Ali and Caroline Hagood, "Heteroglossic Sprees and Murderous Viewpoints in Orhan Pamuk's *My Name is Red*," *Texas Studies in Literature and Language* 54, no. 4 (Winter 2012): 519.

90   For an in-depth discussion of Plato's attitude towards poets and poetry see,Pierre Destrée and Fritz-Gregor Herrmann eds., *Plato and the Poets (Mnemosyne Supplements)* (Leiden/Boston: Brill, 2011), esp. Stephen Halliwell's "Antidotes and Incantations: Is There a Cure for Poetry in Plato's Republic?" 241–266.

91   Pamuk, *My Name Is Red*, 290.

92   Pamuk, *My Name Is Red*, 195.

Conclusion: Beyond the Damaged Nations of East and West

1 Nadeem Aslam, "God and Me," *Granta: the Magazine of New Writing* (Spring 2006), 66–68.
2 Edward Said, *Reflections on Exile and Other Essays* (Cambridge, MA: Harvard University Press, 2000), 171.

Bibliography

Abbas, Sadia. "Leila Aboulela, Religion and the Challenge of the Novel." *Contemporary Literature* 52, no. 3 (2011): 430–461.

Abicht, Ludo, Zayd, Abu Nasr, and Al-Azm, Sadik J. *Islam and Europe: Challenges and Opportunities.* Ithaca: Cornell University Press, 2008.

Abu-Lughud, Lila. "The Muslim Woman: The Power of Images and the Danger of Pity." *Eurozine,* September 1, 2006. http://www.eurozine.com/articles/2006-09-01-abulughod-en.html.

Afaneh, Hisam al-Din Ibn Musa. "To Hit Students, between Ban and Permissibility." http:// www.onislam.net/english/.

Al-Ghazali, Abu Hamid. *Book on the Etiquette of Marriage.* Translated by Madelain Farah. http://www.ghazali.org/works/marriage.htm.

Al-Ghazali, Abu Hamid. T*he Incoherence of the Philosophers.* Translated by Michael E. Marmura. Provo, UT: Brigham Young University Press, 2002.

Al-Ghazali, Abu Hamid. Ihiyaa 'Uluum Al-Diin. Cairo: Daar al-Ma'rifah, no date.

Al-Ghazali, Abu Hamid. *The Jewels of the Qur'an: Al-Ghazali's Theory.* Translated by Muhammad Abul Quasem. Kuala Lumpur: University of Malaysia Press, 1977.

Al-Ghazali, Abu Hamid "Refutation of Philosophy." http://www.ghazali.org/articles/gz1.htm#2.

Ali, Ayaan Hirsi. *Nomad.* Toronto: Vintage Canada, 2011.

Ali, Barish and Caroline Hagood. "Heteroglossic Sprees and Murderous Viewpoints in Orhan Pamuk's *My Name is Red.*" *Texas Studies in Literature and Language* 54, no.4 (2012): 505–529.

Ali, Kecia. "Understanding a Difficult Verse, Qur'an 4:34." *Sisters in Islam, Empowering Voices for Change.* http://www.sistersinislam.org.my/news.php?item.42.46.

Al-Kassim, Dina. "The Faded Bond: Calligraphesis and Kinship in Abdelwahab Meddeb's *Talismano.*" *Public Culture* 13, no. 1 (2001): 113–138.

Allied Media Corporation. "On the Muslim American Market." *Allied Media Corporation.* http://www.allied-media.com/AM/.

Almas, Esra. "Framing *My Name is Red*: Reading a Masterpiece." In *Global Perspectives on Orhan Pamuk: Existentialism and Politics,* edited by Mehnaz M. Afridi and David M. Buyze, 75–90. New York: Palgrave Macmillan, 2012.

Almond, Ian. *The New Orientalists: Postmodern Representations of Islam from Foucault to Baudrillard*. New York: I.B. Tauris, 2007.

Al-Tabari, Abu Ja'far Muhammad Ibn Jarir. *Tafsīr Al-Tabari*. Vol. 8. (Cairo: Maktabat Ibn Taymiyya, no date).

Alterinfo. "Ramadan vs Meddeb 'Collatéral "Pourquoi, désormais, on ne peut plus discuter avec Abdelwahab Meddeb (vidéo du débat sur de FR3)." *Alterinfo.com*, February 3, 2008. http://www.alterinfo.net/Ramadan-vs-Meddeb-Collateral-Pourquoi-desormais-on-ne-peut-plus-discuter-avec-Abdelwahab-Meddeb-video-du-debat-sur-de_a16 466.html.

Amira, Dan. "It's Time to Play Bush, Obama Or Imam?" *NY Magazine*, September 1, 2010. http://nymag.com/daily/intel/2010/09/its_time_to_play_bush_obama_or.html.

Anderson, Benedict. *Imagined Communities: Reflection on the Origin and Spread of Nationalism*. London: Verso, 2006.

Arendt, Hannah. *The Human Condition*. Chicago: University of Chicago Press, 1998.

Arendt, Hannah. *The Origins of Totalitarianism*. Orlando: Benediction Books, 2009.

Arkoun, Muhammad. *Islam: To Reform Or to Subvert*. London: Saqi Books, 2006.

Arkoun, Muhammad. *Rethinking Islam: Common Questions, Uncommon Answers*. Translated and edited by Robert D. Lee. Colorado: Westview Press, 1994.

Arkoun, Muhammad. "Rethinking Mediterranean Space." *Diogene Unesco* 206, (2004).

Arnold, Thomas. *Painting in Islam: A Study of the Pictorial Art in Muslim Culture*. New York: Dover, 1965.

Asad, Talal. *Formations of the Secular: Christianity, Islam, Modernity*. Stanford, California: Stanford California Press, 2003.

Asad, Talal. *Genealogies of Religion: Discipline and Reason of Power in Christianity and Islam*. Baltimore: The Johns Hopkins University Press, 1993.

Asad, Talal. "Historical Notes on the Idea of Secular Criticism." *The Immanent Frame: Secularism, Religion and the Public Sphere* (blog). http://blogs.ssrc.org/tif/2008/01/25/historical-notes-on-the-idea-of-secular-criticism/.

Asad, Talal. "Reflections on Laïcité and the Public Sphere." *Items and Issues*, Social Sciences Research Council 5, no. 3 (2005): 1–11.

Asad, Talal, Wendy Brown, Judith Butler, and Saba Mahmoud. *Is Critique Secular? Blasphemy, Injury and Free Speech*. Los Angeles: The

Townsend Centre for the Humanities, University of California, Berkeley, 2009.

Aslam, Nadeem. "God and Me." *Granta: The Magazine of New Writing*, Spring 2006: 66–68.

Aslam, Nadeem. *Maps for Lost Lovers*. London: Faber and Faber, 2004.

Aslan, Reza. *Not God but God*. New York: Random House Trade Paperback Editions, 2006.

Balibar, Etienne. "Citizen Subject." In *Who Comes After the Subject?*, edited by Eduardo Cadava, 33–57. New York: Routledge, 1991.

Balibar, Etienne. *Masses, Classes, Ideas: Studies on Politics and Philosophy before and After Marx*. Translated by James B. Swenson. New York: Routledge, 1994.

Bangstad, Sindre. "Contesting Secularism/s. Secularism and Islam in the Work of Talal Asad." *Anthropological Theory* 9, no.2 (2009): 188-208.

Bangstad, Sindre. "Saba Mahmood and Anthropological Feminism after Virtue." Theory, Culture and Society 28, no. 3 (May 2011): 28–54.

BBC News. "Pope Sorry for Offending Muslims." *BBC News*. http://news.bbc.co.uk/2/hi/europe/5353208.stm.

Bellah, Robert. *The Robert Bellah Reader*, edited by Robert Bellah and Steven M. Tipton. Durham: Duke University Press, 2006.

Benjamin, Walter. "On the Concept of History." *Creative Commons (Attribute and ShareAlike)*. http://www.marxists.org/reference/archive/benjamin/1940/history.htm.

Benslama, Fethi. "The Veil of Islam." *Journal of the Jan Van Eyck Circle for Lacanian Ideology Critique* 2, (2009): 14–27.

Benslama, Fethi. Psychoanalysis and the Challenge of Islam. Translated by Robert Bonnono. First edition, Minneapolis: University of Minnesota Press, 2009.

Berman, Paul. *The Flight of the Intellectuals*. Brooklyn, New York: Melville House, 2010.

Bloch, Ernst. *The Principle of Hope. Studies in Contemporary German Social Thought*. Vol. 1,2,3. Cambridge, MA: MIT Press, 1995.

Bogus, Anthony. "And what about the Human?: Freedom, Human Emancipation, and the Radical Imagination." *Boundary 2*, 39, no.3 (2012): 29–46.

Borzoi Reader Online, The. "A Conversation with Orhan Pamuk." *Randomhouse.com*.http://www.randomhouse.com/knopf/authors/pamuk/qna.html.

Bourget, Carine. ""9/11 and the Affair of the Muslims Headscarf in Essays by Tahar Ben Jelloun and Abdelwahab Meddeb." *French Cultural Studies* 19, (2008): 71–84.

Brace, Marianne. "Nadeem Aslam: A Question of Honour." *The Independent*, June 11, 2004. http://www.independent.co.uk/arts-enter-tainment/books/features/nadeem-aslam-a-question-of-honour-6167858.html.

Brown, Wendy. "Civilizational Delusions: Secularism, Tolerance, Equality." *Theory and Event* 15, no.2 (2012).

Bruckner, Pascal. "Enlightenment Fundamentalism Or the Racism of the Anti-Racist." *Signandsight.com: Let's talk European.* http://www. signandsight.com/features/1146.html.

Bruckner, Pascal. *The Tears of the White Man: Compassion as Contempt.* Translated by William R. Beer. New York: The Free Press Division, A Division of Macmillan Inc, 1986.

Bruckner, Pascal. *The Tyranny of Guilt: An Essay on Western Masochism.* Translated by Steven Randall. Princeton: Princeton University Press, 2010.

Calhoun, Craig, Mark Juergensmeyer, and Jonathan Van Antwerpen, eds. *Rethinking Secularism.* Oxford: Oxford University Press, 2011.

Casanova, Jose. "Beyond European and American Exceptionalism." In *Predicting Religion,* edited by Grace Davie, Paul Heelas, and Linda Woodhead, 17–29: Hampshire, UK Ashgate Publishers, 2003.

Casanova, Jose. "The Politics of Nativism: Islam in Europe, Catholicism in the United States." *Philosophy and Social Criticism* 38, nos. 4–5 (2012): 485–495.

Casanova, Jose. "Religion, European Secular Identities and European Integration." *Eurozine,* July 29, 2004. http://www.eurozine.com/articles/2004-07-29-casanova-en.htm.

Casanova, Jose. "The Secular, Secularizations, Secularisms." In *Rethinking Secularism,* edited by Craig Calhoun, Mark Juergensmeyer and Jonathan Van Antwerpen, 54–74. Oxford: Oxford University Press, 2011.

Castoriadis, Cornelius. *The Imaginary Institution of Society, [L'institution imaginaire de la societe].* Translated by Kathleen Blamey. Cambridge, MA: MIT Press, 1998.

Cesari, Jocelyn. "Islam in France: The Shaping of a Religious Minority." In *Muslims in the West: From Sojourners to Citizens,* edited by Yvonne Yazbeck Haddat. New York: Oxford University Press, 2002.

Cesari, Jocelyn. *When Islam and Democracy Meet: Muslims in Europe and the United States.* New York: Palgrave Macmillan, 2004.

Chebel, Malek. *Enciclopedie De l'amour En Islam: Érotisme, Beauté, Sexualité Dans Le Monde Arabe, En Perse Et En Turquie.* Paris: Edition Payot, 1993.

Chebel, Malek. *L'imaginaire Arabo-Musulman.* Paris: Presses universitaires de France, 1993.

Çiçekoğlu, Feride. "A Pedagogy of Two Ways of Seeing: A Confrontation of "Word and Image in *My Name is Red.*" *The Journal of Aesthetic Education* 37, no.3 (2003): 1–20.

Connolly, William. *The Ethos of Pluralization*. Minnesota: University of Minnesota Press, 1995.

Courville, Mathieu. *Edward Said's Rhetoric of the Secular*. London: Continuum, 2010.

Dalrymple, William. "The Muslims in the Middle." *The New York Times*, August 16, 2010. http://www.nytimes.com/2010/08/17/opinion/ 17dalrymple.html? _r=1&pagewanted=1.

Declaration of Independence, The. *About.com*, http://usgovinfo.about. com/bldecind.htm.

Destrée, Pierre and Fritz-Gregor Herrmann, eds. *Plato and the Poets (Mnemosyne Supplements)*. Leiden/Boston: Brill, 2011.

Donner, Fred. *Narratives of Islamic Origins: The Beginnings of Islamic Historical Writing*. Princeton. NJ: The Darwin Press, 1998.

El-Badawi, Emran. "Nasr Hamid Abu Zayd: A Film Screening at AUC," *Iqlid*, http://iqlid.wordpress.com/2013/02/18/nhazauc/

El Fadl, Khaled M. Abou. *And God Knows the Soldiers: The Authoritative and the Authoritarian in Islamic Discourse*. Lanham: University Press of America, 2001.

El-Effendi, Abdelwahab. "The People on the Edge: Religious Reform and the Burden of Western Muslim Intellectual." *Harvard Middle Eastern and Islamic Review* 8 (2009): 19–50.

Ess, Josef Van. *The Flowering Muslim Theology [Premices de la Theologie Musulmane]*. Translated by Jane Marie Todd. Cambridge, MA: Harvard University Press, 2006.

Eteraz, Ali. *Children of Dust: A Portrait of a Muslim as a Young Man*. New York: HarperOne, 2009.

Fadel, Muhammad. "Muslim Reformists, Female Citizenship and the Public Accommodation of Islam in Liberal Democracy." In *Politics and Religion* Cambridge: Cambridge University Press, 2012. http://ssrn.com/abstract=1727457

Fadel, Muhammad. "The True, the Good and the Reasonable: The Theological and Ethical Roots of Public Reason in Islamic Law." *Canadian Journal of Law and Jurisprudence* 21, nos. 1–65 (2008).

Fekete, John. "Literature and Politics/ Literary Politics." *Dalhousie Review*, 66.1–2 (1986): 45–86.

Fitzpatrick, Peter. "The Desperate Vacuum: Imperialism and Law in the Experience of Enlightenment." In *Post-Modern Law: Enlightenment, Revolution and the Death of Man*, edited by Anthony Carty, 90–106. Edinburgh: Edinburgh University Press, 1990.

Frank, Richard. *Al-Ghazali and the Asharite School*. Durham, NC: Duke University Press, 1994.

Freedom and Justice Foundation. http://www.freeandjust.org/ Events .htm.

Friscolani, Michael. "At the Shafia Honour Trial the Verdict is in: Guilty."

McLean Magazine, January 29, 2012. http://www2.macleans. ca/2012/01/29/shafia-family-found-guilty/.

Garton Ash, Timothy. "Islam in Europe." *New York Review of Books*, October 5, 2006. http://www.nybooks.com/articles/archives/2006/ oct/05/islam-in-europe/

Gauchet, Marcel. *La Révolution Des Droits De l'homme*. Paris: Gallimard, 1989.

Gourgouris, Stathis. "Antisecularist Failures: A Counterresponse to Saba Mahmood." *Public Culture* 20, no. 3 (2008): 453–459.

Gourgouris, Stathis. "De-Transcendentalizing the Secular." *Public Culture* 20, no. 3 (2008): 437–445.

Gourgouris, Stathis. *Does Literature Think? Literature as Theory for an Antimythical Era*. Stanford: Stanford University Press, 2003.

Gourgouris, Stathis. "Lessons in Secular Criticism, Thinking Out Loud 2012, Three Lectures." University of Western Sydney. http://www.uws.edu.au/philosophy/philosophy@uws/events/thinking_ out_loud/2012.

Gourgouris, Stathis. "On Self-Alteration." *Parrhesia* no. 9 (2010): 1–17.

Gourgouris, Stathis. "The *Poiein* of Secular Criticism." In *A Companion to Comparative Literature*, edited by Ali Behdad and Dominic Thomas, 75–87. West Sussex, UK: Blackwell Publishing Ltd, 2011.

Gourgouris, Stathis. "Transformation, Not Transcendence." *Boundary 2* 31, no.2 (2004): 55–79.

Gourgouris, Stathis. "*Žižek*'s Realism." In *Slavoj Žižek: The Reality of the Virtual, DVD, produced by Ben Wright (2007; Olive Films)*.

Guardian, The. "Trial of Turkish Author Adjourned." *The Guardian*. http://www.guardian.co.uk/world/2005/dec/16/turkey.books.

Habermas, Jürgen. *Justification and Application: Remarks of Discourse Ethics*. Translated by Ciaran P. Cronin. Cambridge, MA: MIT Press, 1993.

Habermas, Jürgen. *Structural Transformations of the Public Sphere*. Translated by Thomas Burger with the assistance of Frederic Lawrence. Cambridge, MA: MIT Press, 1991.

Habermas, Jürgen. *Theory of Communicative Action: Lifeworld and: A Critique of Functionalist Reason*. Translated by Thomas McCarty. Boston: Beacon Press, 1987.

Habermas, Jürgen. *The Theory of Communicative Action: Reason and the Rationalization of Society*, vol. 1. Translated by Thomas McCarty. Boston: Beacon Press, 1984.

Hanggi, Christian. "The Greatest Work of Art. Karlheinz Stockhausen and 9/11" (Lecture, Interventions Symposium at Cabaret Voltaire, Zurich, July 31, 2011). http://web.archive.org/web/ 20060829003224/http://www.danskmusiktidsskrift.dk/doku/stock-hausen-16sep2001.mp3.

Harrington, Austin. "Habermas and the Post-Secular Society." *European Journal of Social Theory* 10, no.4 (2007): 543–560.

Harrison, Victoria S. "Hermeneutics, Religious Language and the Qur'an." *Islam and Christian–Muslim Relations* 21, no. 3 (2010): 207–220.

Holy Father, The. "Faith, Reason and the University – Memories and Reflections." Lecture, Liberia Editrice Vaticana. http://www.vatican.va/holy_father/benedict_xvi/speeches/2006/september/documents/hf_ben-xvi_spe_20060912_university-regensburg_en.html.

Ifex, "International PEN Calls for Government Condemnation of Attacks on Author Orhan Pamuk." *Ifex*. http://www.ifex.org/turkey/2005/04/06/international_pen_calls_for_government/.

Jones, Allison. "All 3 Guilty in Shafia Murder Trial; Judge Condemns Twisted Concept of Honour." *The Canadian Press*. http://ca.news.yahoo.com/shafia-jury-enters-second-full-day-deliberations-kingston-090532874.html.

Kant, Immanuel. "An Answer to the Question what is Enlightenment? 1784." http://www.english.upenn.edu/~mgamer/Etexts/kant.html.

Kant, Immanuel. *Groundwork of the Metaphysics of Morals*. Translated by H. J. Paton. New York: Harper & Row, 1964.

Kesler, Musa. "Nobel Laureate Orhan Pamuk Gets Fined." *Hurriyet Daily News*, March 27, 2011. http://www.hurriyetdailynews.com/default.aspx?pageid=438&n=orhan-pamuk-will-pay-compensation-for-his-words-court-decided-2011-03-27.

Khatibi, Abdelkebir. *La Blessure De Nom Propre*. Paris: Édition Denoël, 1986.

Khoury, Adel Theodore. *Manuel II Paléologue, Entretien Avec Un Musulman (7e Controverse)*. Paris: Edition de Cerf, 1966.

Kidd, James. "Nadeem Aslam. Interview." *Asia Literary Review* 11 (Spring 2009). http://www.asialiteraryreview.com/web/article/en/24.

Koselleck, Reinhard. *The Practice of Conceptual History: Timing History, Spacing Concepts*. Translated by Todd Samuel Presner. Stanford: Stanford University Press, 2002.

Landes, Richard. "Judith Butler and the Adorno Prize: A Preliminary Annotated Bibliography." *The Augean Stables*. http://www.theaugeanstables.com/2012/09/13/judith-butler-and-the-adorno-prize-a-preliminary-annotated-bibliography/.

Lange, Christian. *Justice, Punishment and the Medieval Muslim Imagination*. Cambridge: Cambridge University Press, 2008.

Lazreg, Marnia. *Questioning the Veil: Open Letters to Muslim Women*. Princeton: Princeton University Press, 2009.

Lincoln, Bruce. "Bush's God Talk." *The Christian Century*, October 5, 2004. 22–29.

Lowy, Michael. *Fire Alarm: Reading Walter Benjamin's "On the Concept of History."* London: Verso, 2006.

Lumbard, Joseph. *Submission, Faith and Beauty: The Religion of Islam.* Louisville, KY: Fons Vitae, 2009.

MacAskill, Ewen. "God Told Me to End the Tyranny in Iraq." *The Guardian*, October 7, 2007. http://www.guardian.co.uk/world/2005/oct/07/iraq.usa.

Mahmood, Saba. *Politics of Piety: The Islamic Revival and the Feminist Subject.* Princeton: Princeton University Press, 2005.

Mahmood, Saba. "Secular Imperatives." *Public Culture* 20, no. 3 (2008): 461–465.

Mahmood, Saba. "Secularism, Hermeneutics and Empire: The Politics of Islamic Reformation." *Public Culture* 18, no. 2 (2006): 323–347.

Makdisi, George. *The Rise of Humanism in Classical Islam and the Christian West: With Special Reference to Scholasticism.* Edinburgh: Edinburgh University Press, 1990.

Makdisi, George. "Scholasticism and Humanism in Classical Islam and the Christian West." *Journal of the American Oriental Society* 109, no.2 (1989): 175–182.

Martin, Richard, Mark Woodward, and Dwi S. Atmaja, eds. *The Defenders of Reason in Islam: Mut'azilism from Medieval School to Modern Symbol.* London, England: One World Publication, 1997.

Marx, Karl. "Introduction to the Contribution to the Critique of Hegel's *Philosophy of Right*." In *Karl Marx, Frederick Engels: Collected Works*, vol. 3. Translated by Richard Dixon et al. New York: International Publishers, 1975.

Mas, Ruth. "Love as Difference: The Politics of Love in the Thought of Malek Chebel." *European Review of History* 11, no.2 (2004): 273–301.

Meddeb, Abdelwahab. "La Burqa Est Absente De Qur'an." *Nouvel Observateur*, January 28, 2010. http://tempsreel.nouvelobs.com/actualite/societe/20100128.OBS5145/la-burqa-est-absente-du-coran.html.

Meddeb, Abdelwahab. "Human Rights, Divine Rights." (Conference paper) Universality of Human Rights Forum, Oslo, 21–22 October 2010. http://forumoslo.fede.org/textes/en/AbdelwahabMeddeb_Human_rights_DivineRight_EN.pdf

Meddeb, Abdelwahab. *Islam and its Discontents: An Interview with Frank Berberich.* Translated by Pierre Joris. *October 99* (Winter 2002): 3–20.

Meddeb, Abdelwahab. *The Malady of Islam [La Maladie de L'Islam].* Translated by Pierre Joris and Anne Reid. New York: Basic Books, 2003.

Meddeb, Abdelwahab. *Phantasia.* Paris: Sindbad, 1986.

Meddeb, Abdelwahab. "Pourquoi Ecrivez-Vous." *Libération*, special issue (March, 1985).

Meddeb, Abdelwahab. *Talismano*. Paris: Christian Bourgois, 1979.

Mehrez, Samia. "Translation and the Postcolonial Experience: The Francophone North-African Text " In *Rethinking Translation*, edited by Lawrence Venuti, 120–138. London: Routledge, 1992.

Meisami, Julie and Paul Starkey Scott, eds. *Encyclopedia of Arabic Literature*. Vol. 2. New York: Routledge, 1998.

Mincheva, Dilyana. "'Critical Islam': Debating/Negotiating Modernity." *Journal of Religion and Society, the Kriepke Center* 14 (2012). http://moses.creighton.edu/jrs/2012/2012-18.pdf.

Mincheva, Dilyana. "Western Muslim Intellectuals in Dialogue with Secularism: From Religion to Social Critique." *The International Journal of Religion and Spirituality in Society* 2, no.1 (2012): 13–24.

Mishra, Pankaj. "The Wilderness of Solitude." *New York Review of Books*, June 23, 2005. http://www.nybooks.com/articles/archives/2005/jun/23/the-wilderness-of-solitude/?pagination=false.

Mitha, Farouk. *Al-Ghazali and the Ismailis: A Debate on Reason and Authority in Medieval Islam*. New York: I.B. Tauris, 2002.

Monninger, Michael. "Interview with Abdelwahab Meddeb, Islam's Heritage of Violence." *Die Ziet*, September 21, 2006.

Moosa, Ebrahim. "The Debts and Burdens of Critical Islam." In *Progressive Muslims: On Justice, Gender and Pluralism*, edited by Omid Safi, 111–127. Oxford: One World Publications, 2003.

Morgan, John. "Beyond Ethical Theism: Islamic Morality as a Service to God." *Contemporary Islamic Studies. A Qatar Foundation Academic Journal* (May 2011): 1–5.

Mufti, Aamir R. "The Aura of Authenticity." *Social Text* 18, no.3 (2000): 87–103.

Nancy, Jean-Luc. "Church, State, Resistance." Chap. Part I, In *Political Theologies: Public Religions in a Post-Secular World*, edited by Hent de Vries and Lawrence E. Sullivan, 102–112. New York: Fordham University Press, 2006.

Nobelprize.org, "The Nobel Prize in Literature 2006." *Nobelprize.org*. http://www.nobelprize.org/nobel_prizes/literature/laureates/2006/.

Orthodox Church of New York. "Information Regarding the Cordoba Iniative and the Islamic Community Center in Lower Manhattan." *Orthodox Church of New York*, August 27, 2010. http://nycathedral.org/news.php?id=31.

Pamuk, Orhan. *My Name is Red*. Translated by Erda G knar. London: Faber and Faber, 2001.

Panagia, Davide. *The Poetics of Political Thinking*. Durham: Duke University Press, 2006.

Panagia, Davide. *The Political Life of Sensation*. Durham: Duke University Press, 2009.

Peters, J.R.T.M. *God Created Speech: Study in the Speculative Theology of the Mu'tazili Qadi I-Qudat Abu-l-Hasan Abd Al-Jabar Ibn Ahmad Al-Hamadani*. The Netherlands: Brill Academic Publishers, 1976.

Peters, Rudolph. *Crime and Punishment in Islamic Law: Theory and Practices from the Sixteenth to the Twenty-First Century*. Cambridge: Cambridge University Press, 2005.

Plato. *The Republic: Book X*. Translated by Benjamin Jowett. *The Internet Classics Archive*. http://classics.mit.edu/Plato/republic.11.x.html, 595b.

Procter, James. "A Portrait of Nadeem Aslam." *British Council Literature*. http://literature.britishcouncil.org/nadeem-aslam.

Rahman, Ambadur. "Ground Zero Mosque Imam Helped Bush Administration." *Politics.Gather*, August 19, 2010. http://politics.gather.com/viewArticle.action?articleId=281474978455454.

Rainsford, Sarah. "Authors Trial Set to Test Turkey." *BBC News Istanbul*. http://news.bbc.co.uk/2/hi/europe/4527318.stm.

Ramadan, Tariq. "Ce Que Je Crois: Le Dernier Livre De Tariq Ramadan." http://oumma.com/spip.php?article976.

Ramadan, Tariq. *Islam, the West and the Challenge of Modernity*. London: The Islamic Foundation, Tra Edition, 2009.

Ramadan, Tariq. "Radical Reform: Ethics and Liberation." http://www.tariqramadan.com/article.php3?id_article=1242&lang=en.

Ramadan, Tariq. *Radical Reform: Islamic Ethics and Liberation*. Oxford: Oxford University Press, 2009.

Ramadan, Tariq. *To Be a European Muslim*. Leicester: Islamic Foundation, 1999.

Ratzinger, Joseph and Jürgen Habermas. *The Dialectics of Secularization: On Reason and Religion*. San Francisco: Ignatius Press, 2007.

Rauf, Feisal Abdul. "Justification and Theory of Sharia Law: How the American Declaration of Independence, Bill of Rights and Constitution are Consistent with Islamic Jurisprudence." *University of St. Thomas Law Journal* 7, no.3 (2010): 452–510.

Rauf, Feisal Abdul. "Sharing the Core of our Beliefs." *Common Ground News Service: Constructive Articles that Foster Dialogue*, March 31, 2009. http://www.commongroundnews.org/article.php?id=25141.

Rauf, Feisal Abdul. *What's Right with Islam: A New Vision for Muslims and the West*. New York: HarperCollins, 2005.

Rose, Jacqueline. "A Piece of White Silk." *London Review of Books* 31, no. 21 (November 5, 2009). http://www.lrb.co.uk/v31/n21/jacqueline-rose/a-piece-of-white-silk.

Rosen, Stanley. *Hermeneutics as Politics*. New York: Oxford University Press, 1987.

Rosen, Stanley. *The Quarrel Between Philosophy and Poetry: Studies in Ancient Thought*. New York: Routledge, 1988.

Saeed, Abdullah. *The Qur'an: An Introduction*. New York: Routledge, 2008.

Sahih Muslim. "Book 17, Hadith Number 4206." http://www.hadithcol-lection.com/sahihmuslim/145-Sahih%20Muslim%20Book%2017.%20Punishments%20Prescribed%20By%20Islam/12549-sahih-muslim-book-017-hadith-number-4206.html.

Said, Edward. *Orientalism.* New York: Vintage, 1979.

Said, Edward. *Reflections on Exile and Other Essays.* Cambridge, MA: Harvard University Press, 2000.

Said, Edward. *The World, the Text and the Critic.* Cambridge, MA: Harvard University Press, 1983.

Salvatore, Armando. "Authority in Question: Secularity, Republicanism, and 'Communitarianism' in the Emerging Euro-Islamic Public Sphere." *Theory, Culture and Society* 24, no.2 (2007): 135–160.

Scott, David and Charles Hirschkind, eds. *Powers of the Secular Modern: Talal Asad and His Interlocutors.* Stanford: Stanford University Press, 2006.

Shaikh, Nermeen. *The Present as History: Critical Perspectives on Contemporary Global Power.* New York: Columbia University Press, 2007.

Shaikh, Sa'diyya. "Exegetical Violence: Nushuz in Quranic Gender Ideology." *Journal for Islamic Studies* 17 (1997): 49–73.

Shinikov, Atanas. *To Flog Or Not to Flog: What a Question is it. On Instructive Uses of Violence in Sources of Islamic Pedagogy and Education.* PhD dissertation, Sofia University St. Kliment Ohridski.

Singer, Brian. *Society, Theory and the French Revolution.* London: Macmillan, 1989.

Soroush, Abdel Karim. "Text in Context, Lecture Delivered at McGill University, Institute of Islamic Studies, April 13, 1995." In *Liberal Islam: a sourcebook,* edited by Charles Kurzman. Oxford: Oxford University Press, 1998.

Stein, Sam. "Ground Zero Mosque Imam Helped FBI with Counterterrorism Efforts." *The Huffington Post,* August 17, 2010. http://www.huffingtonpost.com/2010/08/17/ground-zero-imam-helped-f_n_685071.html.

Stockhausen, Karlheinz. "Huuuh!" *Musiktexte* 91 (2002): 69–77.

Szerman, Nathalie. "Tunisian Reformist Abdelwahab Meddeb: It's Up to the Arab to Take the Courageous Step of Questioning His Faith." In *Arab Watch for Reformation and Democracy,* January 24, 2007. http://www.awrd.net/look/en-article.tpl?IdLanguage=1&IdPublication=1&NrArticle=1570&NrIssue=2&NrSection=6.

Taymiyya, Ibn. *Fatawa Ibn Taymiyya.* Mansoura: Dar-al-Wafa' li-l-ila'a wal-Nashr, 2005.

Taylor, Charles. *A Secular Age.* Cambridge, MA: Belknap Press of Harvard University Press, 2007.

Taylor, Charles. "A Secular Age: Buffered and Porous Selves." *The*

Immanent Frame (blog). September 2, 2008. http://blogs.ssrc.org/tif/2008/09/02/buffered-and-porous-selves/.

The Centre for Islamic Sciences. "Muhammed Arkoun." *The Center for Islamic Sciences.* http://cis-ca.org/voices/a/arkoun.htm.

The Immanent Frame. "Is critique secular?" *The Immanent Frame* (blog). http://blogs.ssrc.org/tif/category/is-critique-secular/.

Timeous of Plato, in Five Books, Containing a Treasury of Pythagoric and Platonic Physiology. Vol. 1. Translated by Thomas Taylor. London: Walworth, Surrey, 1820.

Walleckx, Tristan. "Naissance Médiatique De l'Intellectuel Musulman En France (1989–2005)." MA Thesis, Université Montpellier 3, 2005). http://www.memoireonline.com/12/05/63/m_naissance-intellectuel-musulman-medias-francais2.html.

Warner, Michael, Jonathan Van Antwerpen, and Craig Calhoun, eds. *Varieties of Secularism in a Secular Age.* Cambridge, MA: Harvard University Press, 2010.

Weinberg, Steven. "Without God." *New York Review of Books,* September 25, 2008. http://www.nybooks.com/articles/archives/2008/sep/25/without-god/?pagination=false (accessed February 20, 2013).

Whitehead, Kenneth. "Mistaken National Identity: Samuel Huntington's Who Are We." *The Catholic Science Review* 10 (2005): 197–214.

Wolfe, Gregory. "East and West in Miniature." *Image* 53 (Spring 2007).

Wolin, Sheldon. *Politics and Vision: Continuity and Innovation in Western Political Thought.* Princeton, NJ: Princeton University Press, 2004.

Zayd Nasr, Abu. "The Dilemma of the Literary Approach to the Qur'an." *Alif: Journal of Comparative Poetics* 23, no. Literature and the Sacred (2003): 8–47.

Zayd, Nasr Abu. "The Qur'an: God and Man in Communication." Inaugural Lecture, November 27, 2000, Leiden University. http://www.let.leidenuniv.nl/forum/01_1/onderzoek/lecture.pdf.

Zayd Nasr, Abu. *Reformation of Islamic Thought: A Critical Historical Analysis.* Amsterdam: Amsterdam University Press, 2006.

Zeitlin, Irving. *The Historical Muhammad.* Cambridge, UK: Polity Press, 2007.

Žižek, Slavoj. *The Puppet and the Dwarf: The Perverse Core of Christianity.* Cambridge, MA: MIT Press, 2003.

Index

Abbas, Sadia, 114
Abbas, Sheikh, 46
Abdelkarim, Farid, 46
Abdul Rauf, Mahmoud, 17
Abel (Habil), 93–4, 95
Abraham, 39, 42, 48, 49, 87
Abu Bakr Siddiq, 91
Abu Dawuud, 16, 133*n*
Abu Nuwas, 20, 81
Abu Zayd, Nasr
  death of, 33
  God of Islam, 35, 36
  Islamic reform, 45
  Mahmood's criticism of, 54, 59, 60
  Mut'azilite school of Sunni Islam, 34
  Qur'an as a human text, 60
  Quranic hermeneutics, 15, 25, 32, 34–6, 53, 75–6, 106, 136*n*
  secularization of the Qur'an, 34, 35–6
Ackermann, Ulrike, 68
Afaneh, Hisam al-Din Ibn Musa, 15–16
Afghanistan
  Soviet invasion, 81
  Taliban, 75, 125
Ahmad (d. 885), 133*n*
Al-Qaeda, 82
Ali, Ahmed, 36
Ali, Ayaan Hirsi, 65–8, 69, 72
Almohad Caliphate, 80
Almoravid dynasty, 80
Amara, Fadela, 46, 72
Americanization, 81
Anas bin Malik, 17
Anderson, Benedict, 29

anthropological analysis, 38–9
  see also Asad, Talal; Chebel, Malek; Mahmood, Saba
Arab Spring revolutions, 127
Arab-American News, 76
arabesques, 81, 125
Arendt, Hannah, 30
Arkoun, Muhammad
  death of, 33
  Franco-Maghrebi population, 45
  God of Islam, 39
  hijab affair, 33
  Islamic fact, 38
  Islamic reason, 38
  plurality of Islam, 38
  Qur'anic definition of man, 38–9
  Quranic fact, 38
  Quranic hermeneutics, 15, 25, 32–3, 38–40, 53, 106, 136*n*
artistic creation, 99–100
Asad, Talal
  criticism of critical Islam, 53
  Enlightenment project, 27, 28
  krisis and *parrhesia*, 26–7
  the secular, 26, 57, 58, 59, 61
  secularization, 27, 28
Ash'arites, 34, 137*n*
Asharq Al-Awsat, 75
Aslam, Nadeem, 77–8
  "God and Me" essay, 125
  guilt topic, 107–8
  honour killings, 98, 102–4
  idolatry, 125
  Islamic background, 15
  literary style, 99, 100–1
  Maps for Lost Lovers, 18, 78, 98–9, 100–6, 107–8
  new media technologies use, 77